Trading Places

Trading Places

The East India Company and Asia 1600–1834

Anthony Farrington

THE BRITISH LIBRARY

Trading Places: The East India Company and Asia
An exhibition at The British Library
24 May – 15 September 2002

Sponsored by  Standard
Chartered

In association with **The Daily Telegraph**

First published 2002 by
The British Library
96 Euston Road
London NW1 2DB

British Library Cataloguing in Publication Data
A catalogue record for this book is available from The British Library

ISBN 0 7123 4756 9

Designed and typeset by Andrew Shoolbred
Maps by John Mitchell
Printed in Spain by Grafos S.A., Barcelona

Contents

To Kirti Narayan Chaudhuri,
an archivist's inspiration

Sponsor's Foreword

Standard Chartered is delighted to be sponsoring the exhibition *Trading Places: The East India Company and Asia* at The British Library.

Standard Chartered is today the world's leading emerging markets bank, with operations in over 50 countries in Africa, the Middle East, Asia and the Americas. The earliest roots of Standard Chartered date from three banks formed in the nineteenth century to serve the growth of trade throughout the British Empire. The Chartered Bank of India, Australia and China was founded in 1853 with the grant of a Royal Charter by Queen Victoria. The Standard Bank of British South Africa began trading in 1862. Grindlay Co. was established by Captain James Grindlay, previously with the East India Company, in 1828. Standard Bank and Chartered Bank merged in 1969, and Grindlays was acquired in 2000 to form today's Standard Chartered.

At the heart of the long history of the Group has been the development of free trade following the abolition of the East India Company's monopolies in India in 1813 and in China in 1833. Chartered Bank opened its first branches in India and China in 1858, in Singapore in 1859, Indonesia in 1867 and in Malaysia in 1875.

Today, Standard Chartered is 'a' if not 'the' leading international bank in these markets – and in many other countries in Africa, the Middle East and Asia. As these markets develop – and growing affluence leads to a demand for mortgages, credit cards, personal loans, trade finance and treasury services – the bank will continue to build on the courageous, creative and truly international legacy of the East India Company.

Sir Patrick Gillam
Chairman

Mervyn Davies
Group Chief Executive

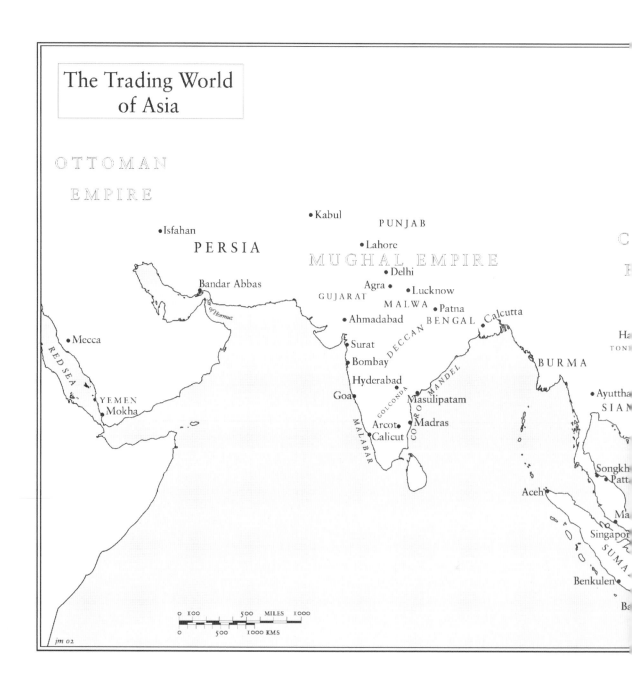

The Trading World of Asia

OTTOMAN

EMPIRE

• Kabul

PUNJAB

• Isfahan

PERSIA

MUGHAL EMPIRE

• Lahore

• Delhi

Agra • • Lucknow

GUJARAT

MALWA • Patna

Calcutta

• Ahmadabad

BENGAL

Bandar Abbas

Strait of Hormuz

• Mecca

• Surat

DECCAN

BURMA

RED SEA

• Bombay

Hyderabad

Ha

TON

YEMEN

Goa•

GOLCONDA

CORO MANDEL

• Masulipatam

• Ayuttha

SIAM

Mokha

MALABAR

Arcot• • Madras

•Calicut

o

Songkh

•Patt

Aceh•

Ma

Singapor

SUMA

Benkulen•

Ba

0   100   500   MILES   1000

0   500   1000 KMS

jm 02

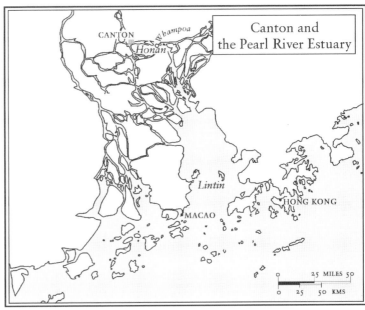

Canton and the Pearl River Estuary

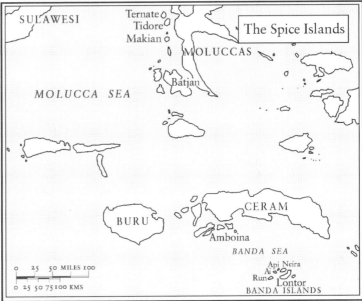

The Spice Islands

The Beginning

The site is now almost deserted, a few buildings and ruins scattered over the countryside of Java's north coast, a day trip west out of the sprawl of modern Jakarta. From the white stone minaret of a red-tiled mosque the sea can be glimpsed beyond rice fields. Nearby are the tombs of the Sultans. Among the broken walls of the royal palace enclosure fragments of Chinese porcelain still lie underfoot.

Four hundred years ago this was Bantam, one of the great port cities of Asia, and it was here that two small ships of the English East India Company arrived in December 1602.

The Company of Merchants of London trading into the East Indies had been founded by a charter from Queen Elizabeth I on 31 December 1600, following more than a year of political negotiations and finance raising. The charter named 218 subscribers to the new enterprise, which was to be managed by a Governor and twenty-four Directors (rather confusingly called 'committees') and which was granted a monopoly of all English trade in any lands lying east from the Cape of Good Hope to the Straits of Magellan – in other words, the whole of Asia and the Pacific. This kind of restriction on competition was typical of late Elizabethan overseas trade, given the risks involved. Earlier examples were the Muscovy Company of 1555, trading through the Baltic to Russia, and the Levant Company of 1580, trading to the Ottoman world. Both had shown an interest in exploring overland routes to Asia, but it was the Dutch who were to provide the immediate spur for an English Company.

The exotic luxury products of the inexhaustible treasure house of Asia – pepper, spices, medicinal drugs, aromatic woods, perfumes and silks – had been trickling into Europe for centuries. The Roman Empire

Bantam, looking towards the sea from the minaret of the Great Mosque.

Photograph by the author

had contact with India by sea and with China by overland caravan routes. Constantinople, the successor to Rome, traded east and by the thirteenth century Venice had become its prosperous middleman. Early travellers, like the Franciscan missionaries to the Mongols and later Marco Polo, brought some knowledge of countries as far away as China into the European consciousness, embellishing their accounts with the fabulous and the wonderful. Although Constantinople fell to the Turks in 1453, an accommodation was reached and the trading interface between Asia and Europe continued to be located in a now completely Islamicised eastern Mediterranean.

Why were spices so important in Asia and Europe, and why were merchants willing to travel great distances and take great risks to obtain them? They gave taste and flavour to otherwise bland foods, they were mixed, blended and distilled into medicines and perfumes, and their rarity made them extremely valuable. Trading in them offered the possibility of making a fortune.

Pepper, the most common spice, added 'heat' to food throughout India and China, and in Europe, for those wealthy enough to afford it, disguised the brine-preserved meat of the winter months. Cloves, grown only in the Banda and Molucca islands of Indonesia, were used for flavouring, perfumes and medicines – a clove pomander could mask the stench of inadequate sanitation and unwashed bodies, while clove oil remains a welcome antidote to toothache. Grated nutmeg was widely used in sweet dishes. Both the nut and the fibrous mace which surrounds it yielded expensive oils for perfumery and drugs. Cinnamon bark, ginger root, galangal and cardamom similarly had their culinary and pharmaceutical applications.

While Venice still dominated the trade, on the western edge of Europe Portugal had begun to explore south into the Atlantic and along the coasts of Africa. Bartolomeu Dias rounded the Cape of Good Hope in 1487 but was forced to turn back. In 1498 Vasco da Gama crossed the Indian Ocean to the port of Calicut on the Malabar coast, opening the 'sea route to the Indies'. At roughly the same time Spain, following the first voyage of Columbus, had irrupted into the new world of the Americas.

The maritime trading world of Asia that the Portuguese entered covered the whole of the Indian Ocean and the China Seas. The annual rhythms of the monsoon winds linked Arabia, Arab East Africa, the Gulf and Persia to western India, carried Arab, Persian and Indian traders across the Bay of Bengal and into Southeast and East Asia, and brought junks from the ports of South China.

Early in the fifteenth century China had embarked on a great venture into the Indian Ocean. Between 1405 and 1433 seven trading fleets of more than 300 'treasure ships' at a time, some of them up to 400 feet long, with crews totalling 28,000 men, ranged the seas from Taiwan to modern Kenya under the eunuch admiral Zheng He, symbolising the power and authority of the Ming Emperor. Internal political conflicts, together with renewed threats of Mongol invasion, ended the experiment and the Chinese state turned away from the outside world.

The meeting point between the Indian Ocean and the China Seas became the southern end of the Malay peninsula and the islands of Indonesia, the source of spices, to which ships from the west and junks from the north could sail and return with the winds of a single year. Malacca, on the eastern side of the straits leading from the Indian Ocean, rose to power and wealth as the great emporium of inter-Asian trade. Its Muslim rulers offered the essential ingredients of peaceful access to all comers, whatever their race or religion, as well as predictable customs duties, legally enforceable contracts, secure warehousing and standard weights and measures.

The Portuguese brought with them the concept of aggressive armed trading in ships carrying heavy guns. Theirs was a national enterprise, fuelled not only by the drive for personal and national wealth but also by their long struggle against Islam and their zeal to spread Christianity. Within ten years they had experienced the weakness of Indian shipping, they had evaded the only serious combination against them, an Egyptian-Calicut alliance in 1509 which fell apart through the defection of the Sultan of Gujarat, and they were beginning to enforce their grandiose claim to be 'Lords of the Sea' in the Indian Ocean.

Goa, halfway between Calicut and Gujarat, was seized in 1510. Malacca was captured in 1511, followed by Hormuz at the entrance to

Asia noviter delineata, published at Amsterdam by William Blaeu, c.1640. Maps like this, while conveying the latest information in wonderfully decorative form, were of no practical use in sailing to Asia. Seamen relied on hard experience supplemented by written sailing directions, known as rutters, which the Portuguese always attempted to keep secret.

British Library, Map Collection: C.5. b.1

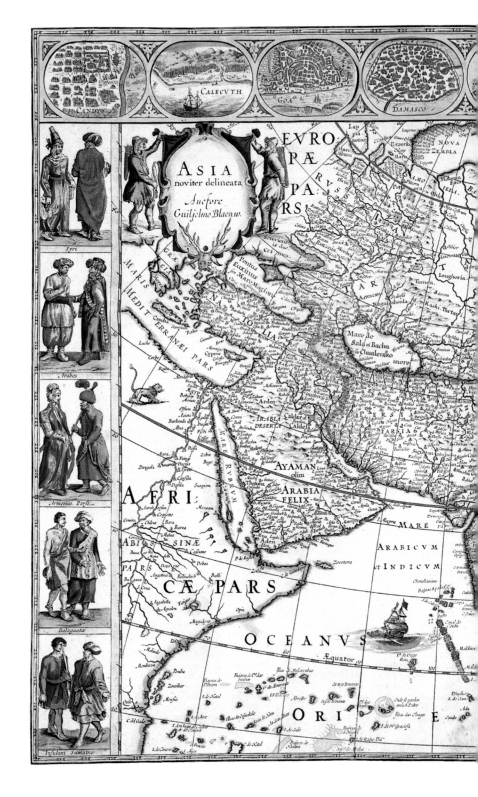

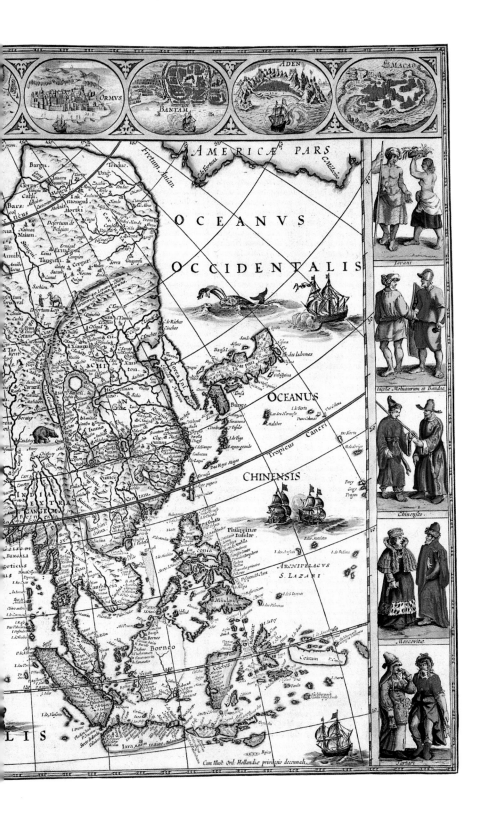

the Gulf in 1515, and a series of fortified posts was established along the east coast of Africa. There was no single great power in the Indian Ocean capable of resisting the Portuguese guns. Although the Mughals were consolidating an empire in northern India from the late 1520s, it was nearly fifty years before their conquests brought them to the sea coasts of Gujarat and Bengal.

Conditions in East Asia were very different. The Chinese state could have squashed them at any time, but because it had prohibited all contact with Japan in response to continual Japanese pirate raids on its coasts, around 1557 China chose to permit a strictly controlled Portuguese settlement at Macao, near Canton, which came to fulfil the useful function of trading Chinese silks for Japanese silver. As Japan evolved a strong central authority after a long period of warlordism, the Portuguese were similarly allowed to settle at Nagasaki from 1571. In both countries their profile was that of the peaceful merchant.

Everywhere the Portuguese went they were accompanied by the Catholic church, especially the Jesuit 'Soldiers of Christ'. Conversions were relatively few, except by force at Goa and, remarkably, by persuasion in Japan, where the Jesuits played a leading role in the Macao–Nagasaki trade as a way of financing their Christian endeavour. Meanwhile the Spaniards, who had crossed the Pacific from Mexico to establish a base at Manila in the 1570s, brought Franciscan and Dominican missionaries to the field. By 1600 there were more than 200,000 Japanese Christians, but as the Japanese state came to see the converts as potentially subversive, it embarked on a series of persecutions and horrific martyrdoms, and then expelled the Portuguese in 1639.

Lisbon, at the end of a chain of sea coast settlements stretching to the other side of the world, became the new terminus for the products of Asia. Great purpose-built ships called carracks sailed east each year and for almost a century Portugal alone developed an expertise in managing trade over such vast distances in time and space, and accumulated knowledge of the countries and peoples of Asia. The distribution of Asian imports from Lisbon was mainly in the hands of the Dutch, who had the largest merchant fleet in Europe after long experience in the North Sea and Baltic fisheries.

In 1578 the young King Sebastian of Portugal, full of Catholic fervour, launched an invasion of Morocco. He and his army were totally destroyed, leaving the succession to the crown unsecured until Philip II of Spain stepped in to unite Spain and Portugal in 1580. Portugal's overseas trading interests, especially its homeward-bound carracks in the Atlantic, were fair game for Spain's Protestant enemies – the now rebellious Dutch fighting for independence in the former Spanish Netherlands, and the England of Elizabeth. Francis Drake returned from his voyage around the world in 1580, during which he had visited the spice islands of Indonesia; in 1588 the Spanish Armada was beaten off; in 1591 James Lancaster, in search of Portuguese ships to plunder, penetrated the Indian Ocean as far as Aceh at the northern tip of Sumatra; in 1587 and 1592 the rich cargoes of the carracks *San Filippe* and *Madre de Dios*, both captured off the Azores, were sold in London.

It was the Dutch who launched the first trading challenge in Asia. Through their long association with Portugal they had been able to collect sailing directions and maps, and in their former position as inter-mediaries in the spice trade out of Lisbon they had gained invaluable commercial knowledge. Dutch Catholics who had served the Portuguese in Asia were another asset. Dirk Gerritszoon's notes on navi-gation as far as China were included in a Leiden publication of 1592, the *Tresoor der Zeevaert*, and in the same year Jan Huyghen van Linschoten returned home after sixteen years in Goa. His *Itinerario*, published between 1594 and 1596, discussed the routes, countries, peoples and products, lavishly illustrated with engraved plates and up-to-date maps.

The first Dutch trading voyage of 1595 returned with a cargo of pepper from Bantam in the summer of 1597. Its experiences appeared in print in an illustrated *Historie van Indien*, published at Amsterdam in 1598, and in the same year a translation of Linschoten's work was issued in London. During the course of 1598 various Dutch cities fitted out twenty-two ships in a race to join the new trade. Over the next three years there were forty more. In 1602 these separate ventures came together in a United East India Company, the Vereenigde Oostindische Compagnie, or VOC for short.

The first subscription list for the English East India Company, 22 September 1599.

British Library, OIOC: B/1, f.6

The threat to England's Levant trade was obvious and spurred on the formation of the Company of Merchants of London trading into the East Indies. The first subscription list, of 22 September 1599, when preparations for an English voyage were well under way, had 101 names, at least twenty-three of whom were Levant Company merchants. After the Company was formed its first Governor, Sir Thomas Smythe, was

VERA EFFIGIES PRÆCLARISS.ᵐᵢ. VIRI DOM. ᵢₙ. THOMÆ SMITH / EQVITIS AVRATI ETC.

The Honourable Sᵣ Thomas Smith Knight, late Embaſ-ador from his Maᵗⁱᵉ to yᵉ great Emperour of Ruſſie, Gouernoue of yᵉ Honᵇˡᵉ and famous Societyes of Marchaⁿᵗˢ tradinge to yᵉ East-Indies, Muſcovy, the French and Somer Ilands Company: Treſurer for Virginia. etc.

Simon Paſſeus ſculp: Lond: Aᵒ 1616. Jo: Woodall excudit.

Sir Thomas Smythe, first
Governor of the East India
Company, engraved by Simon
de Passe, London, 1616.
British Library, OIOC: P1489

also Governor of the Levant Company. The total sum eventually subscribed was £68,373, a massive amount for a relatively poor country like England. It is difficult to translate the figure into a modern equivalent, but at roughly the same date a skilled craftsman like a stonemason or a carpenter could expect to earn around 7 pence for a day's work.

The Ships

Four ships were purchased for the first English voyage to the East – the *Dragon*, *Hector*, *Ascension* and *Susan*, under the command of James Lancaster, carrying nearly 500 men and 110 guns. There was also a small supply ship called the *Gift*, which was set adrift in the Atlantic once its stores had been used. Leaving Woolwich on 13 February 1601, the fleet was delayed in the Channel until 20 April, lost a month becalmed on the Equator, and reached the Cape of Good Hope on 9 September. More than 100 men had already died. After recuperating in Table Bay for seven weeks they sailed again, going ashore on the coast of Madagascar and in the Nicobar islands before arriving at Aceh in June 1602, sixteen months out from London.

The *Susan* was sent down to the pepper-producing areas in the south of Sumatra, while Lancaster turned to his old trade of seeking Portuguese ships to plunder. Luck was on his side. Joined by a Dutch ship, in the Straits of Malacca on 3–4 October 1602 he fought and captured a 1200 ton Portuguese carrack, the *Santo Antonio*, carrying a rich cargo from the west coast of India. After returning to Aceh, the *Susan* and *Ascension* were sent home with pepper. Lancaster sailed with the *Dragon* and *Hector* for Bantam, arriving on 16 December 1602. Two months were spent in loading the ships with pepper, and at his departure in February 1603 Lancaster left behind three merchants and eight other men to assemble a cargo for future English arrivals. All four ships reached England in safety by September 1603. The English East India Company had been launched.

Between 1604 and 1613 eleven more 'voyages' left London's River Thames. The destination of all of them was Bantam, although other ports began to be visited from as early as 1608. Each of the voyages was

The arms used by the East India Company until 1709, a plaster cast of a ceiling boss in Poplar Chapel, East London.
British Library, OIOC: F859

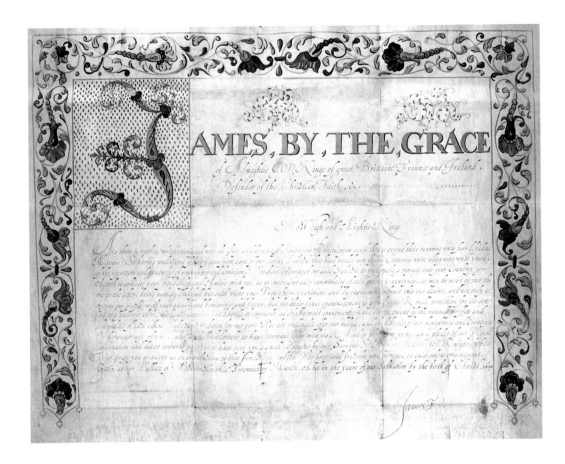

Letter from King James I to an Asian ruler, 30 March 1619, carried by Sir Henry Middleton in the East India Company's Sixth Voyage. The letter, which has a blank space for a name to be inserted as appropriate, was returned to England unused.

British Library, Manuscript Collections: Add.Ch.56456

separately financed by a subscription raised from the English East India Company's members and its accounts were wound up when the cargoes of the returning ships had been sold. The most profitable was the 1612 voyage, which gave subscribers their money back plus 220% profit. After 1613 the Company moved to a system of subscribing to joint stocks, running over a number of voyages or a period of years, and eventually to a single permanent stock whereby investors became shareholders in the Company itself rather than the success or failure of particular voyages. Members could buy and sell shares at the current market price and, like a modern company, the profits realised were devoted to running costs, re-investment, and the payment of annual dividends to shareholders.

The Company's success was an important element in the development of London as a financial and shipping centre, but at first the perspective from Asia was rather different. The English were yet another group of foreigners arriving in ports which had long been accustomed to dealing with foreigners. They were perhaps stranger than most, certainly they had travelled greater distances, and their manners were doubtful. Their heavily armed ships might prove a nuisance or, as enemies of the Portuguese, they might prove useful. The English presence could serve to drive up demand and increase prices, while their gifts and customs payments were as welcome as those of any other merchant group.

Over the whole trading life of the Company, from 1600 to 1833, about 4600 ship voyages were made from London. Between 1620 and 1700 sailings averaged eight ships a year. After 1800 the average was forty-two a year, of much greater individual tonnage. All this activity made the Company England's (and later Britain's) single biggest commercial enterprise. In terms of the total volume of Asian maritime trade it was never more than a tiny percentage.

Shipyard model of the East Indiaman *Charles Grant*, 1252 tons, 26 guns, built at Bombay in 1810 for the trade between London and China.

National Maritime Museum: 1810–14

Blackwall Yard on the River
Thames, by Francis Holman,
1784.

National Maritime Museum:
1935–49

The early ships were bought from a number of different sources.
In 1614 the Company purchased land at Blackwall on the Thames, at
the north-east corner of the Isle of Dogs, excavated a dock, and began
to build its own ships under the direction of William Burrell of Ratcliff.
As early as 1639 the Company started to experiment with hiring ships
instead of building them and this option, which avoided tying up
capital in depreciating assets (four voyages to Asia over a period of eight
to ten years was the expected life of a wooden hull) as well as saving the
shipyard running costs, became the norm. The Blackwall yard was
finally sold in 1656 and thereafter only a handful of ships actually
belonged to the Company.

Blackwall and other yards on the Thames continued to build
specifically for the East India trade on the understanding that the ships
would be freighted by the Company at fixed rates for a specified number
of voyages. The finance was provided by groups of managing owners –
usually taking a one-sixteenth share each – who were also responsible
for supplying the crews. Many owners were also Directors or other major
shareholders of the Company and the 'shipping interest' became a

powerful lobby in its affairs. The ships were operated according to a charter-party, a formal contract between the Company and the owners, setting out the ports of call, the time to be spent in port and the cargoes to be loaded, with financial adjustments to the freight terms for changes made in Asia or for breaches of the contract such as over-staying in port or carrying illicit cargo.

Conditions on board were always cramped, unsanitary and difficult. The ships were rarely more than about 120 feet/36.6 metres long and 35 feet/10.7 metres wide (by the 1800s they had only increased to about 170 x 45 feet/52 x 13.7 metres) and needed crews of 100 plus to carry out the complicated business of operating the sails and to man the guns when need arose. Officers and important passengers had the privileges of cabin space and better food, while the seamen were herded together below decks on a diet which gradually worsened as a voyage progressed and the stores began to deteriorate.

The list of provisions for the 280 officers, merchants and seamen on two ships and a small pinnace sent out in 1606 is typical. It consisted of hard-baked bread and flour (24 lbs/10.9 kgs of each per man per month), weak beer, strong beer, cider (2 pints/1.12 litres of each per man per day), wine (1 pint/0.57 litres per man per day), dry salted beef and pickled beef (1½ lbs/0.68 kgs per man per day for two months and four months respectively), pickled pork (4 lbs/1.8 kgs per day between five men for ten months), dried peas, dried beans, dried cod and other dried fish, oatmeal, wheat in the husk (which was boiled into a kind of porridge), and 78 tons/79.2 tonnes of water. 'Extraordinary victuals' included cheese, butter, 1120 gallons/5091.5 litres of olive oil, vinegar, strong spirits, honey, rice, salt, candles, lamp-oil, wine for the captain's table, and lemon juice as an antidote to scurvy. Fresh vegetables, fruit, meat and water were, of course, taken on whenever a ship touched land, but for most seamen stinking water, rotten flesh and weeks or months on short rations were routine. Later ships carried live animals out from England, slaughtering them for the officers' meals. Fresh fish, surprisingly, played little part in a seaman's diet – the English ate meat, even if it was putrid.

Entry of a death in the log of the East Indiaman *Rochester*, 5 April 1712.

British Library, OIOC: L/MAR/B/137B, p.181

OPPOSITE Title page of John Woodall's *The Surgions Mate*, London, 1617.

British Library, C123.e.9

Some ships made the round trip of at least eighteen months with few deaths on board. Others suffered greatly from fatigue brought on by foul weather and illness caused by foul provisions. Seamen were a tough breed, but even their natural immunities could not cope with the unknown diseases lurking in Asian ports. The 'flux', or dysentery, was common, in its more extreme and deadly forms described as the 'bloody flux', while fevers and aching limbs were characterised as the 'ague'. Against 'tertian ague' (malaria), cholera, typhoid and the plague there were no effective remedies.

Showing a creditable concern for the welfare of their men, from 1614 until his death in 1643 the Company employed John Woodall of St Bartholomew's Hospital in London to oversee the competence of surgeons appointed to the ships and to advise on suitable medicines and instruments for each surgeon's chest. In 1617 he published *The Surgions Mate*, a practical guide to operations such as tooth-drawing,

THE
SVRGIONS
MATE,
OR
A TREATISE DISCO-
uering faithfully and plainely the due
contents of the SVRGIONS *Chest*, the *vses of the*
Inſtruments, the vertues and operations of the
Medicines, the cures of the moſt frequent
diſeaſes at SEA:

Namely

Wounds, Apoſtumes, Vlcers, Fiſtulaes, Frac-
tures, *Diſlocations*, with the true maner of *Amputation,*
the cure of the *Scuruie*, the Fluxes of the belly,
of the *Collica and Illiaca Paſſio, Tenaſmus,*
and exitus Ani, the *Callenture;*

WITH A BRIEFE EXPLANATION
of *Sal, Sulphur*, and *Mercury*; with certaine
Characters, and tearmes of *Arte*.

Publiſhed chiefly for the benefit of young Sea-Surgions,
imployed in the *Eaſt-India* Companies affaires.

By *Iohn Woodall* M.r in Chirurgery.

LONDON
Printed by EDWARD GRIFFIN for *Laurence Liſle*,
at the *Tygers-head* in *Pauls Church-yard*. 1617.

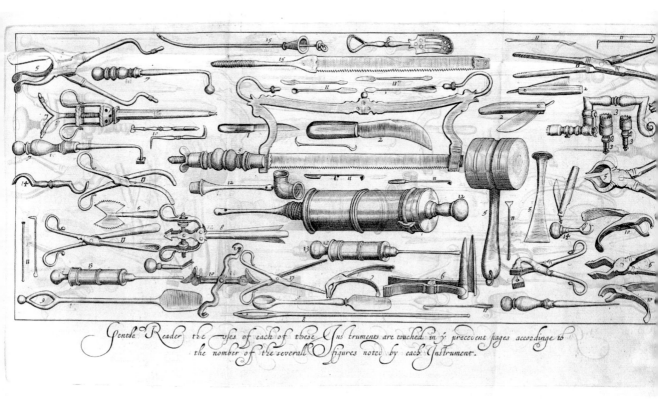

Gentle Reader the uses of each of these Instruments are touched in y precedent pages accordinge to
the number of the severall figures noted by each Instrument.

Seventeenth-century surgical
instruments, from the 1639
edition of Woodall.

British Library, C77.h.18

blood-letting and the amputation of limbs with the 'dismembring saw'.
It proved so useful that new editions appeared in 1639 and 1655.

Another instance of welfare concerns was a fund set up in 1627 to
assist deserving seamen maimed or grown old in the Company's service,
or their widows and orphans. Almshouses were built at Poplar, close to
Blackwall, providing pensioners with accommodation and 2½ pence
per day for their food. Even on this modest allowance drunkenness and
misbehaviour were perennial problems. The first two pensioners, John
Fern and Tristram Hughson, admitted on 5 March 1628, were not
untypical. Hughson, who had lost a leg at sea, was frequently drunk and
in that state would complain bitterly against the Directors and other
gentlemen. Fern was told on admission that he could not take his wife
to live with him, so he took another man's wife instead, had children by
her and eventually married her although her husband was still alive. He
was ejected in 1634. After receiving a number of donations from

Company members who had grown wealthy in the trade, the charity came to be financed by small deductions from each seaman's wages. A chapel for the pensioners and the inhabitants of Poplar was completed in 1654. Both survived until 1866, when the almshouses were demolished and the chapel, reconstituted as the parish church of St Matthias Poplar, was largely rebuilt. Today, dwarfed by the Canary Wharf skyscrapers of a revitalised London Docklands, it serves as a local community centre.

A few ships had chaplains on board, but in general acts of worship – Sunday services and burials at sea – were left to the captain. Indeed, after the Navigation Acts of the 1660s stipulated that English vessels with crews in excess of 100 should carry chaplains, ships hired by the Company were invariably registered as 99 crew. From the late seventeenth century a handful of chaplains were also employed to serve the spiritual needs of the staff in the Company's trading settlements, but they were strictly forbidden to attempt any kind of missionary activity among the surrounding Asian communities.

The greatest danger which the seamen faced was shipwreck, though losses were in fact infrequent. Only 231 of the Company's 4600 separate sailings between 1600 and 1833 ended in disaster, 5% of the total; 110 are reported wrecks and 32 simply disappeared at sea, victims of hurricanes or other violent storms. The remainder were lost to enemy action, mainly Dutch or French, or were destroyed by fire or explosion through carelessness with candles and cooking stoves, or the mishandling of gunpowder. The Company could afford to be relatively sanguine and after a few experiments in the 1630s and 1640s it did not insure its cargoes. Ship owners had the choice of covering their risk on the developing London marine insurance market.

Tragedies at sea, with stories of great suffering and heroism, captured the public imagination and were disseminated in the eighteenth and nineteenth centuries by immediate publication. One of the most famous was the wreck of the *Grosvenor*, lost on 4 August 1782 on the South African coast north of modern Durban, when Captain John Coxon incorrectly estimated that he was 300 miles from the nearest land. There were 123 survivors, who set off to walk along the shore to the Dutch settlements at the Cape, over a thousand miles away. The ever hopeful Captain Coxon declared that sixteen days march should suffice. Constantly harassed by Africans, who stripped them of anything of value, the group split up into smaller parties. After 117 days six seamen reached an outlying Dutch post 300 miles east of the Cape. A subsequent search party found ten more seamen and two passengers. All the rest disappeared. Because the *Grosvenor* was known to be carrying 720 bars of gold, 1400 bars of silver and nine boxes of precious stones, the legend of its treasure lingered powerfully in South Africa and inspired many fruitless salvage projects, some of them little more than money-raising swindles.

The *Sussex*, homeward bound from China with a cargo that included thousands of pieces of porcelain, was battered by gales off Madagascar, lost her mainmast and had a great depth of water in the hold. On 9 March 1738 Captain Francis Gostlin decided to abandon his ship, transferring the crew to the nearby, less badly damaged *Winchester*. However, Seaman John Dean and fifteen other members of the crew refused to leave. Remarkably they were able to steer the *Sussex*, carrying only a few sails, into St Augustine's Bay on Madagascar, where they effected some repairs and then attempted to sail her for Mozambique – but the ship hit the dreaded Bassas da India reefs in the middle of the Mozambique Channel. Dean and four others survived, escaping to a rocky islet. They managed to salvage a damaged ship's boat and then made a seventeen-day voyage back to Madagascar. Only Dean lived to return to London. He appeared before the Company's Directors on 2 September 1741 to be commended for his devotion to duty. He was rewarded with a pension for life of £100 a year as well as a post as foreman of the Company's Drug Warehouse in London, and sat for his portrait by the artist Willem Verelst. He also had the satisfaction of seeing Captain Gostlin pursued in the courts and bankrupted by an award of £25,000 damages against him.

With ships leaving London during the winter months to gain the appropriate positions for the timing of the winds in the South Atlantic and the Indian Ocean, coasts nearer to home claimed their share of victims. A fierce gale blew the *Halsewell* broadside onto the cliffs at

John Dean, by William Verelst, c.1743.

British Library, OIOC: F19

Seacombe in Dorset on 6 January 1786. Nearly 200 lives were lost, mostly dashed to pieces on the rocks while attempting to swim ashore. The passengers included Captain Richard Pierce's two daughters aged 17 and 15, his two unmarried nieces and three other single girls, all on their way to find rich husbands in India. Preferring 'perishing with his daughters to being preserved without them', Captain Pierce became a posthumous hero of contemporary prints, sheltering the females in his manly arms as they awaited death.

Through the incompetence of its Channel pilot the *Earl of Abergavenny*, during foul weather on the evening of 5 February 1805, hit the Shambles, a well-known shoal off the Isle of Portland, also in Dorset. The 1200-ton ship got off the rocks but was so badly damaged that despite frantic pumping she slowly sank in the open sea, firing her guns to attract assistance from the shore. A large contingent of recruits for regiments serving in India meant that there were 402 people on board. When the hull touched bottom the topmasts and rigging still appeared above the surface, covered with hundreds of souls desperately clinging on as the waves broke over them. Only 152 were saved. Captain John Wordsworth went down with his ship. His beloved brother, the poet William Wordsworth, was deeply affected by the tragedy for the rest of his life.

When the *Hartwell* hit uncharted rocks off Boa Vista in the Cape Verde Islands on 24 May 1784 two lives were lost, along with bullion amounting to 320,000 Spanish silver dollars. Two expeditions in 1788–89 by the pioneering divers, the brothers John and William Braithwaite, managed to salvage most of the silver. They used the primitive and incredibly dangerous technique of descending in a barrel with an airline connection to a pump on the surface, and from inside it, hand-operated claws to pick up the bullion.

Their modern successors, whether treasure hunters or underwater archaeologists, have the benefit of sophisticated equipment like sonar scanners, magnetometers (used to detect ferrous metal remains of cannon and anchors on the seabed), aqualungs, and suction pumps, though the dangers and difficulties of working below the surface have changed little since the Braithwaite days.

A few Company wrecks have been located and excavated at sites ranging from the north Kent coast to the southern Philippines. As well as 'treasure' in the form of bullion or saleable artefacts, they have provided valuable information on ship construction and such mundane matters as cargo packaging and stowage, while thousands of everyday objects bring a time-capsule immediacy to life on board. The protection of historic British shipwrecks, including the Company's ships, and arrangements for controlled excavation where appropriate, remains a highly contentious and as yet unresolved issue.

The *Earl of Abergavenny*, off Southsea, by Thomas Luny, 1801.

British Library, OIOC: F59

Bantam and the Wider World

Bantam had existed as a city of the Sundanese kingdom of Pajajaran from at least the eleventh century, although it was then located inland, and there is archaeological evidence of early international trading links. Its rise as a great international port, however, took place during the sixteenth century. After they captured Malacca in 1511 the Portuguese began trading south for the abundant pepper of the areas on both sides of the Straits of Sunda, which were already well known to the Chinese. Around 1527 local converts to Islam, aided by the Muslim Sultan of Demak in central Java, seized control, creating a new kingdom with its capital on the coast. The first ruler, Hasanudin, shook off dependence on Demak and at his death in 1570 the kingdom of Bantam comprised most of western Java and southern Sumatra. Despite religious differences, trade with the Portuguese flourished, while the Chinese came in ever increasing numbers. Pepper provided the revenues for a boom which quickly made the city one of the largest in Southeast Asia.

When the English ships anchored in 1602 they found a central district bounded by two small rivers, surrounded by formidable walls five miles in circumference, enclosing the royal palace, the principal mosque and the houses of the Javanese nobility. Outside the walls on the east the great market was held every day. On the west was a flourishing Chinese quarter, where the English East India Company rented a compound for living quarters and warehouses to establish its first 'factory' in Asia – the term, which was used by all the Europeans, simply means a place where factors, or representatives of a merchant company, live and trade.

An immediate problem was how to communicate. Serious proficiency in Asian languages was confined to the Jesuits and other Catholic

The great market at Bantam, from Lodewijckszoon, 1598. (*Detail*)

British Library, 1486.gg.18

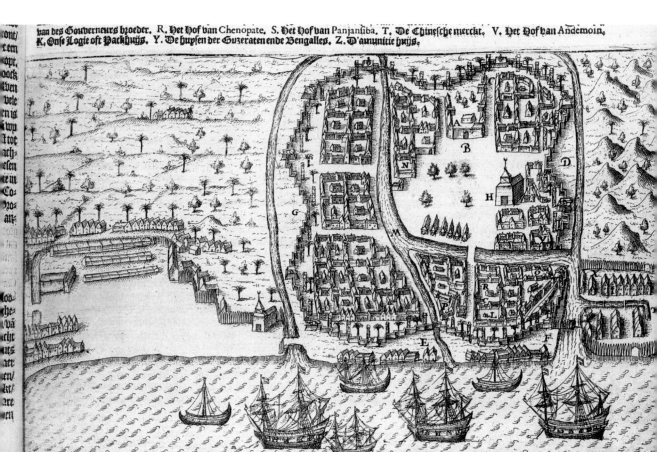
ban des Gouberneurs broeder. R. Het Hof ban Chenopate. S. Het Hof ban Panjanſiba. T. De Chineſche merckt. V. Het Hof ban Andemoin. K. Onſe Logie oft Packhuijs. Y. De huijfen der Guzeraten ende Bengalles. Z. D'amunitie huijs.

Plan of Bantam, from *Historie van Indien* by Willem Lodewijckszoon, published at Amsterdam in 1598. Lodewijckszoon's book, illustrated with 43 plates and 7 maps, describes the first Dutch voyage to the East Indies between 1595 and 1597.

British Library, 1858.a.1 (1)

missionaries. The English found that they could begin with a smatter-ing of Portuguese on both sides, though it was soon replaced by Malay, which the Chinese had used as the *lingua franca* in Southeast Asia long before any Europeans arrived. The very first 'Company publication' entitled *A true and large discourse of the voyage... to the East Indies*, a 34-page pamphlet printed in London in 1603, has a list of 52 Malay words and phrases, starting with the numbers. Other basics include: how sell you?, whither go you?, a ship, a boat, pepper, good, not good. Less usefully, it also has 55 words and phrases in the Mon language, the result of a chance encounter at Aceh with merchants from Lower Burma. It must have been a curious encounter that recorded: breeches, stockings, hair of the head, the moon, a star, a fingernail, a whore, and

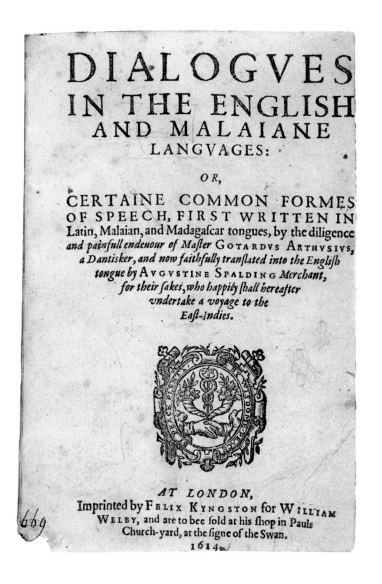

DIALOGVES
IN THE ENGLISH
AND MALAIANE
LANGVAGES:

OR,

CERTAINE COMMON FORMES
OF SPEECH, FIRST WRITTEN IN
Latin, Malaian, and Madagafcar tongues, by the diligence
and painfull endeuour of Mafter GOTARDVS ARTHVSIVS,
*a Dantisker, and now faithfully tranflated into the Englifh
tongue by* AVGVSTINE SPALDING *Merchant,
for their fakes, who happily fhall hereafter
vndertake a voyage to the
Eaft-Indies.*

AT LONDON,
Imprinted by FELIX KYNGSTON for WILLIAM
WELBY, and are to bee fold at his fhop in Pauls
Church-yard, at the figne of the Swan.
1614.

Dialogues in the English and Malaiane Languages, 1614, the first Malay book printed in England.

British Library, G16734 (669)

the verb to spit. In 1614 further assistance was provided by *Dialogues in the English and Malaiane Languages,* a translation by the Company merchant Augustine Spalding of a work derived from Dutch reports by the Danish scholar Gotthard Arthus. When their factories began to spread out beyond the Malay world, the Company gradually adopted the practice of sending out apprentice boys to learn the rudiments of the local language as a prerequisite for employment, while long-term relationships with Asian women and close proximity to Asian employees always provided alternative routes for language learning.

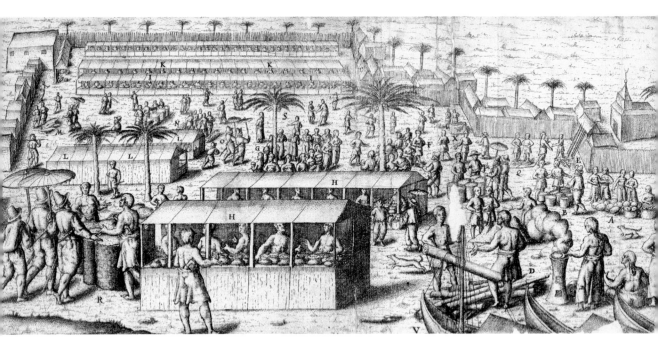

In the great market at Bantam, assisted by local brokers and fixers, the English met Arab, Turkish, Persian, Gujarati, Tamil, Bengali, Malay, Javanese and Chinese merchants, who had all brought with them the products of their own countries. Alongside the ubiquitous pepper, the market bought and sold an incredible range of exotic goods – fine spices from the islands of eastern Indonesia, Chinese silks and porcelain, Japanese lacquer, precious stones, carpets, strange drugs and gourmet foods, dyestuffs, rare gums and essences, scented woods, ingredients for incense and, above all, a bewildering variety of textiles from India.

What did the English have to offer in return? The answer is, very little apart from silver. The first voyage carried out nearly £28,000 worth, the bulk of it Spanish dollars, *reales de plata* or pieces of eight, bought in the European bullion markets. After a century of Portuguese activity the *real* had become generally accepted throughout Asia as a coin of reliable weight and fineness. Indeed, for nearly three hundred years a large percentage of the output of the fabulously rich mines in Spanish Mexico and Peru flowed into Asia, reflecting the long imbalance between high demand in Europe for the sophisticated manufactures and natural products of Asia, and low demand in Asia for anything from Europe.

England's principal manufactures were fine-quality, heavy woollen broadcloth and lighter cloths like kerseys, serges and baize. The very idea of a substantial market for English woollen textiles in the climates of South, Southeast and East Asia seems absurd. It should not be supposed, though, that the Company and its servants were such poor merchants that they did not quickly come to appreciate the difficulties involved. Unfortunately there was little choice. Left to itself it is probable that the Company, after the experience of the first few voyages, would have exported little other than silver; but it was under constant pressure to assist the national economy by creating overseas markets for English manufactures. A condition of the monopoly status the English East India Company held, was the commercially irritating obligation to send out a proportion of its annual export cargoes in goods as opposed to bullion or coin.

OPPOSITE TOP The great market at Bantam, from Lodewijckszoon, 1598. The engraving is accompanied by a key in Dutch, which translates as follows:

A Melons and coconuts
B Sugar and honey for sale in pots
C Bean market
D Bamboo and rattan market
E Place where krises, swords, lances and helmets are sold
F Men's clothes
G Women's clothes
H Stalls for all kinds of spices and drugs
I Stalls of the Bengalis and Gujaratis
K The Chinese stalls
L Meat stalls
M Fish market
N Fruit market
O Fresh vegetables market
P Pepper market
Q Onion and garlic market
R Rice market
S The place where merchants meet
T Jewellers' stalls
V The mooring place for all kinds of boats
X Poultry market

British Library, 1486.gg.18

OPPOSITE BELOW An early encounter with Asian music: Lodewijckszoon's depiction of a Javanese gamelan orchestra, 1598.

British Library, 1858.a.1 (1)

Two bales 2

One bale --- s

One bale --- s

a very light Blew --- five bales --- 5

two bales --- 2

One bale --- s

One bale --- s

three bales --- 3

A perfect clear white --- five bales --- 5

five bales --- 5

a purple --- --- --- five bales --- 5

a Chocolate colour --- five bales --- 5

57½

N: B: All the cloth of the fi
=ness and thinness as y' blac
cloth muster, and to be mad
a good gloss. —

The 20 bales Embost y
same as usualy sent out b
must have a good gloss —

About Sixty to Seventy
=bost Carpetts w'th Borders and
more variety of colours in a
=pet y' more Esteemed of the
length & breadth as follow B

1½ yards Broad & 3 long		3
2	4	10
2½	5	10
3	6	3
3½	7	5
4	8	5
	Carpets --- 6	5

The second half of the seventeenth century saw serious attacks on the Company's monopoly by the clothiers of Gloucestershire and the East Midlands, fronted by Parliamentary spokesmen. The monopoly survived at the cost of a legal obligation to the home manufacturers. The 1693 renewal of the Company's charter that granted them the monopoly ordered an annual export of £150,000 worth of manufactured goods, while William III's re-grant of the charter in 1698 stipulated that 10% of annual exports should consist of English products.

Apart from silver and woollen textiles, available exports were mainly unwrought metals – iron, lead and tin – miscellaneous 'fancy goods' like sword blades, knives and looking-glasses, and re-export items like African ivory or Mediterranean coral. Leaving ship construction and management on one side, perhaps the only areas where there was a technological superiority over Asia were guns, ranging from heavy cannon to the latest muskets, though for obvious reasons they were rarely traded, and eventually the instruments of the new European scientific revolution, from telescopes to humble reading spectacles.

The experience gained at Bantam soon revealed that Asian goods could be bought most profitably by barter for other Asian goods, especially Indian textiles. How to obtain them and how to dispose of English broadcloth were immediate concerns. In August 1608 the *Hector* became the first English ship to reach an Indian port when it arrived at Surat. The follow-up, the 1610 fleet of three ships under Sir Henry Middleton, was ordered away from Surat by its Mughal governor, anxious not to alienate the Portuguese. Middleton took his revenge at the entrance to the Red Sea (where he was joined by John Saris with the main English fleet of 1611) by intercepting the annual Haj pilgrimage ships from Surat. But because they were not 'pirates', in return for thousands of pieces of Indian textiles taken by force from the Gujarati vessels the English cunningly handed over broadcloth, keeping business-like accounts of their transactions, before sailing for Bantam.

At roughly the same time a separate English ship of 1611, the *Globe*, opened relations on the opposite coast of India, outside the territories of the Mughal Empire. A few merchants were left at Masulipatam, the port of the independent Muslim kingdom of Golconda, to

OPPOSITE Samples of English broadcloth suitable for the market at Mokha, 1721.
British Library, OIOC: G/17/1, f.119

begin buying textiles for the Southeast Asian market. The *Globe* went on to Pattani, a transit port for Chinese junks on the north-eastern side of the Malay peninsula, and Ayutthaya, the capital of Siam. The hope was that the factories settled at both places would be able to acquire raw silk and silk textiles from Chinese merchants at cheaper rates than those prevailing at Bantam. The reality was that most of what arrived was pre-empted by agents of the rulers.

Two years later an ambitious East Asia project was launched with the opening of a factory at Hirado in Japan. There were special circumstances behind this leap from Bantam to the north. Firstly, it had been reported that an Englishman, known to influential members of the Company in London, was living in Japan in great favour with its military dictator, the *shogun* Tokugawa Ieyasu (always mistakenly referred to by the Company as the 'Emperor'). William Adams, born at Gillingham, Kent, in 1564, had been apprenticed to Nicholas Diggins of Limehouse on the Thames to learn the arts of shipbuilding and navigation. As a young man he served as a ship's master out of London and took part in Dutch expeditions to the Arctic in search of the North-East Passage. In 1598 he sailed as pilot in a Dutch fleet intended to plunder along the coasts of Chile and Peru before crossing the Pacific to trade in Indonesia. The fleet fell apart after wintering in the Straits of Magellan. One ship, the *Liefde*, eventually reached Japan in April 1600 with only Adams and 23 others left alive. Chosen to represent the crew, Adams survived imprisonment followed by interviews with Ieyasu interpreted by the hostile Portuguese Jesuit João Rodrigues.

When it became clear that the crew would not be allowed to leave – the *Liefde* had been confiscated – each went his separate way in Japan with the help of a small annual pension. Adams, who must have been a man of considerable talents, became a trusted adviser to Ieyasu, supervising the construction of two European-style ships. He was raised to the status of *hatamoto*, or direct retainer of the *shogun*; he was granted an estate south-west of Edo (modern Tokyo); he took a Japanese wife, by whom he had two children; and eventually he replaced Rodrigues as official interpreter for European strangers. In this capacity he helped the Dutch VOC to settle a factory at Hirado in 1609.

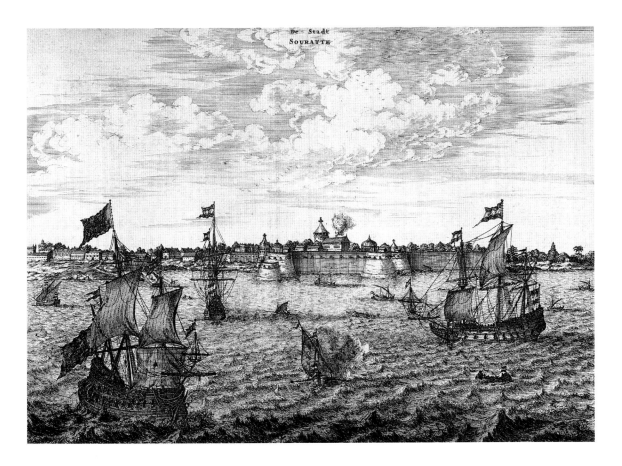

De Stadt
SOURATTE

The second element in the circumstances which began to move trade outwards from Bantam was a business plan for the East Asian region, largely formulated in London. The theory ran that within the monsoons of a single year, ships from Bantam could purchase Chinese silks at mainland Southeast Asian ports like Pattani and Ayutthaya, sell them in Japan for locally produced silver (the Tokugawa regime was successfully exploiting recently discovered mines), purchase return cargoes of pepper and spices for London at Bantam with some of this silver, and carry the rest of it home. The Company would then be able to confound growing criticism that its operations were draining the national wealth.

It was all nonsense, not least because silk was hardly ever available to the English in sufficient volume to enable the theory to succeed on a practical level. When John Saris reached Hirado in 1613 with the ship

The city of Surat, from a Dutch engraving reproduced in John Ogilby's *Asia*, London, 1673.
British Library, 648b.14

The Matsuura family mansion at Hirado, Japan.

Photograph by the author

Clove of the 1611 fleet, he brought with him the usual broadcloth, Spanish dollars and miscellaneous goods, though he did have his share of more marketable Indian textiles taken from the Gujarati ships in the Red Sea episode. The Japan factory, which was closed down ten years later, turned out to be an object lesson in just how much the English Company had to learn about the sophisticated requirements of the Asian markets.

However, Adams assisted the new arrivals at Hirado, while urging that they should settle in Edo Bay, close to the centre of power. Though it was a convenient port for ships coming from the south, much frequented by Chinese junks (and the Portuguese before they moved to

Nagasaki), Hirado lay at the very western edge of Japan, inconveniently far from the main cities and markets. When they met, Saris seems to have taken an instant dislike to Adams, 'a naturalised Japanner' who initially turned up to welcome him dressed as a *samurai*, wearing the two swords of his rank, and ignored Adams's advice about conditions in Japan, to the eventual detriment of the Company.

The Japanese market proved highly dependent upon particular standards of taste and the vagaries of fashion and novelty. Indian textiles 'fantastically painted or striped' sold well at first. A year later the only demand was for patterns of white spots on blue or black grounds. Broadcloth found a tiny niche market as a lining for weapon or armour boxes, or as saddle blankets, but encouraged by Saris when he returned home in 1614 the Company continued to send large quantities to Japan.

Saris's cultural and commercial misreporting, which caused so much trouble for the factory staff, is well illustrated by the example of gallipots. These were cheap glazed earthenware pots, used in England for a variety of purposes ranging from kitchen items to containers for apothecaries' ointments. The Matsuura family, the feudal lords of Hirado, were famous practitioners of their own school of the Zen Buddhist tea ceremony, which deliberately cultivates as part of its ritual the use of sophisticatedly naive ceramics, the more unusual the better. A few gallipots on board the *Clove* must have been seized upon by these warrior connoisseurs, for on 14 November 1614, after he returned to London and reported that cheap pots could be sold for fabulous prices, the Company's Directors instructed Saris to select and purchase varieties of 'stone pots much requested in Japan' from the manufacturers in Southwark. They were sent out to Japan on the *Hosiander* in 1615, but found no sales. The factory accounts for June 1616 reveal that there were then 2161 assorted gallipots lying in the warehouse. Except for a handful given away as presents, the shipment of pots was still there when the factory closed.

The small group of English at Hirado also had an early experience of the sheer scale and magnificence of a major Asian power. The factory chief, Richard Cocks, not only kept a vivid personal diary from 1615

Captayne, Adames and mr. Richard Wickham, vezen
shall. please god to send yow to Edero. or miaco
that yow shmd boreared money for sure good (as
yow carry wth. Eather off the Emperour. or any
other then I pray yow. furnishe the yonge byryer
off friendes some same. noat. a thowsand tais
or wght he stand in want off. in takinge a
boroate off his hand for the repaiment thereof
in firando. at Demand. thus much the said
byryer willed me to write in this note for
the more contentie off his furnishing thereof wth
I pray yow. both shme a care to pforme And
both so comyt yow. to god. From the Englishe
Howse at firando in Zapan the 24th decembr 1613

yow. Loainge friend.
Ric. Cocks.

until 1622 (it survives among the British Library's collections) but also wrote numerous letters to the Company and friends in London attempting to describe the wonders he had seen with his own eyes. Cocks's patron and correspondent Sir Thomas Wilson recorded an audience with King James I in March 1619, when he told him: 'It seemes that neather our cosmographers nor other wryters have given us true relation of the greatnes of the princes of those parts, for of the island of Japan hee tells these strange things following. Warrs wherin 300 thousand men slayne at a tyme. A king's courte of an 100 thousand men continually resident. A king's pallace capable to lodge 200 thousand men, far bigger than your Majestie's citty of York, the citty without three tymes as much more.' Wilson subsequently noted 'His Majesty could not be induced to beleeve that the things written are true, but desyred to speake with the writer when he comes home.' They were true, of course, though Cocks never had the chance to defend his descriptions. Ordered home in disgrace as a scapegoat for the factory's failure, he died at sea in March 1624. Adams spent the rest of his life in Japan. He died at Hirado in 1620, where his story lives on as a great asset to the local Tourist Board.

OPPOSITE Letter from Richard Cocks at Hirado to William Adams and Richard Wickham at Edo, dated 24 December 1613, with Japanese text authorising a loan to the Matsuura feudal lord. Cocks signed his name for the second time with a *fude* or writing brush, presumably handed to him by the Japanese scribe.

British Library, OIOC: E/3/1, no.126

Spices and the Dutch

The Dutch arrived at Bantam in 1596, six years before the English – a pattern that was to be repeated for the next eighty years. Their United East India Company, or VOC, of 1602 began with ten times the capital of the English East India Company and easy access to the manpower of North Germany and the Baltic. Almost everywhere the English Company went in its efforts to purchase Asian goods at source and to compete alongside existing Asian networks of trade, it found the Dutch already there, with more ships, more men, more money and a far more focused national purpose. As early as 1601 the Dutch had demonstrated what lay ahead when they smashed a Portuguese fleet in a full-scale naval battle in the bay of Bantam. Portuguese merchants, whose pepper purchases had been important in the growth of Bantam, abandoned the city.

Cloves sold in Europe for at least three times the price of pepper. Nutmegs and mace were even more expensive. It soon became clear that the newly-formed VOC intended a complete takeover of the European trade in fine spices and that it would do whatever necessary to squeeze out the English Company and the remnants of Iberian influence. The method was both simple and ruthless – to seize control of the sources of production. The spice islands of the Banda group (Lontor, Neira, Api, Ai and Run), the intervening Buru, Ceram and Amboina, and the Moluccas (Batjan, Makian, Tidore and Ternate) were ruled by independent local kings and chieftains, most of them hostile to each other. The VOC embarked on the classic ploy of offering 'protection' against all enemies to individual rulers in return for treaties guaranteeing that their spice crops would be sold only to the Dutch. Selling to others was a breach of treaty, justifying immediate armed occupation. In 1605 the

Agreement with the East India Company for the exclusive purchase of pepper at Silebar in western Sumatra, 16 March 1683. Written in Malay, in Jawi script.

British Library, OIOC: E/3/43, ff.50v–51r

انى صلى الله عليه وسلم شريب حبيبل فى ليسكر ناهى
كفد تاهن باكند بولن ربى ال اول كفد ها رحمت ثلا وقت ظهر
ابن لوغ كباغ دفتى اوجخ طلب بر حيثى دفتى اول لر دفتى
لا ورغ كند دفنى شروتن دوابلس بر حيثى دفنى بلح من كرفة
دفن دانا كوف فى ترك فنى انكر يس لا دولى بر دفنى لا دانق
سوغنى كوبى بر سموات لا دات كفنى اقلر يس بر حبيبى
دى ان فى نا بول بر جول كفد اوخ لا ين مركات سقول سرك بها س

Sellebar 16 March 1662

The above is a Contract made with the Roy de Patte
Ujang gallo, and de Patte Ulobarah, and de Patte
Lauuong, and ye rest of ye Councill for all Peppar
yearly at R[s] 10 pr Bahar.

ابن لوغ تر بلحين دفتى اوجخ بله بر دمنه فى تر بربا با
يخ شكلو كفلا سهار است تا هملخ فر ولد هن دفتى فى شرير
حباير دى

The above is an Obligation given Depate Ujang
Galloe to give him 15 pr Bahar on all Peppar

جكلو سلطان اكرمنتا ببيا كفد اوخ لولي بربنز من كرفة
دقن دانل كوف نز حبا بر دل جكلو دابغ وبلد كسولي بر انق
افكر يس لا دونت اقلر يس دودق دلولي بر

The above is a note given to Depato Ujang Gallo
to beare him harmelesse from ye Old Sultan of
Bantam.

Hon:ble S:rs   Sillebar ye 29 Aprill 1663

The 19 February sailed from Batavia, and ye 6th March
arrived here ye 11th ye Rompsthorne and Surratt Mrchant in
being informed by ye Natives of a great quantity of
Peppar procurable here and ye Placos adjacent, had
great hopes of lading both these Ships or at least
the Surat Mrchant, and in order thereunto applyed our
selues unto ye Govern and great men importuning them
to come to an agrem:t for ye Peppar wch so long in stood
on R[s] 16 ye Bahar, ye thereof being as they preten-
ded or Custome for ye Old Sultan of Bantam and
whose protection they were, and if hould be demanded from them, but after wee had conuinced them of
their error and unreasonable demands in insisting on
ye Old Sultans Custome, when they were sencible hee
had lost hit Cowry, and ye Dutch in Possession thereof,
and answered to seuerall of their impertinent questions
with wch shall not trouble your Hon:rs wee on ye 16th March
came to an agreement for ye Peppar at R[s] 10 ye Bahar,

VOC built a massive fort on the clove island of Amboina, from 1607 the Sultan of Ternate was their puppet, and in 1609 came another large fort on Banda Neira.

English trading attempts were routinely obstructed by Dutch ships, forts and garrisons. They were unable to offer effective counter-protection to the spice producers, indeed any promises made were soon broken and served as pretexts for Dutch reprisals against the island populations. In October 1616, in desperation at what had happened to their world, the Bandanese of Run ceded their island to the English Crown. The VOC moved from threats to open hostilities. Seven English ships were captured and the Company's chief commander, John Jourdain, was killed on the deck of his ship off Pattani by a Dutch sharpshooter during truce negotiations in July 1619.

In the same year the VOC's newly appointed Governor-General, Jan Pieterszoon Coen, took the decision to make their small post at Jacatra, east of Bantam, the main rendezvous for Dutch trade. Javanese resistance was crushed, Jacatra was destroyed, and the castle and city of Batavia began to take shape. Batavia, now Jakarta the capital of Indonesia, became the headquarters of the VOC's operations throughout Asia, in imitation of Portuguese Goa. By 1624 it had a population of 8000. Soldiers, overseas Chinese settlers, migrants from Europe, and slaves bought in Madagascar, India and the islands poured in to create a Dutch colonial settlement.

Meanwhile the English Company had finally managed to put together a large fleet of fifteen ships and was prepared to challenge the VOC. But just as a naval battle was imminent, news arrived in March 1620 that agreement had been reached in Europe for the two Companies to share purchases and expenses in Asia. It reached far-away Run too late to prevent the surrender of the island to the Dutch of Banda Neira, after a siege of more than four years.

A period of half-hearted cooperation ensued. Under the terms of the agreement the English moved from Bantam to Batavia. An ironically mis-named Anglo-Dutch Fleet of Defence came together to attack Portuguese shipping off the west coast of India and to blockade Spanish Manila, where the opportunity was also taken to plunder

Chinese junk traffic. Such cooperation was, of course, totally at odds with Coen's designs and in any case proved short-lived. The English Company could not sustain its share of the expenses and the status of Run remained in dispute, while in 1622 the VOC ships in the combined East Asia fleet launched their own separate, though unsuccessful, attempt to capture Macao.

Worse was to follow. In February 1623 Gabriel Towerson, English chief on the clove island of Amboina, and nine other Company servants (together with nine Japanese *samurai* mercenaries, some of them from Hirado, and a Portuguese) were executed by the Dutch Governor Herman van Speult on a charge of conspiracy to seize the fort there. The proceedings were marked by horrific tortures to extract confessions and it is likely that the 'plot' was a convenient fabrication designed to drive the English permanently out of the spice islands. The news caused uproar in Europe. Pamphlets replete with gory frontispieces and titles beginning *A true relation of the unjust, cruell and barbarous proceedings against the English* appeared in London, to be refuted in turn by publications from Amsterdam, but the affair was never settled and joined that of Run to bedevil Anglo–Dutch relations for two generations. Soon after the English Company withdrew from Japan and from mainland Southeast Asia. An attempt to settle on the island of Lagundy in the Straits of Sunda in 1624 was thwarted by disease and it was not until 1628 that the English shook themselves free from Dutch supervision and moved back to Bantam.

Direct access to the spice islands was firmly closed. The English concentrated on the pepper trade of Bantam and southern Sumatra, while at the same time opening contact for fine spices with Makassar, on the south-western arm of Sulawesi, whose intrepid Bugis seafarers continued to visit the islands in defiance of the Dutch. This loophole was not closed until 1667, when the VOC occupied Makassar and forced its ruler to exclude all other Europeans.

Bantam and Batavia continued an uneasy relationship, punctuated by the VOC capture of Malacca in 1641 and the three Anglo–Dutch Wars of 1652–54, 1665–67 and 1672–74. Whatever their outcomes in Europe, in Asia the English invariably saw their ships captured and their Bantam trade interrupted. The Treaty of Breda at the end of the second war did, though, resolve the problem of Run. In return for the British Crown relinquishing its claim to Run, the Dutch handed over their New Netherlands settlement, based on the island of Manhattan, which had long been an irritant to the colonists of New England.

The final VOC triumph came in 1682. Abu'l Fatah, the 'old' Sultan of Bantam, who had resigned his throne under pressure from his son Sultan Abdul Kahar two years before, resumed the government by force. Abdul Kahar, under siege in Bantam, appealed to Batavia. On 28 March 1682 the city fell to VOC Governor-General Cornelis Speelman's forces. Fulfilling one of the conditions for Dutch assistance, the English factory was ordered out and its personnel evacuated Bantam on 11 April. News of their expulsion reached London in mid-March 1683. Preparations to meet force with force began but were soon abandoned, and it looked as if the VOC would succeed in excluding its rival from the trade in Indonesian pepper as well as fine spices.

Pepper had been the most important single commodity of the Company's trade for most of the seventeenth century. The quantities imported were enormous, for instance more than 7,000,000 lbs/ 3,175,200 kgs in 1677, and much of what was sold in London was re-exported to markets as far away as Poland, Russia and the Ottoman Empire. Although profit margins were small, the sheer volume of the trade coupled with its historic associations as the 'foundation commodity' made the English determined to keep market share as a matter of national pride and a sign of resistance to the VOC's ambitions.

Most of the pepper shipped from Bantam originated in southern Sumatra. Efforts to find an alternative regular supply were now concentrated there. In 1685 the English negotiated a settlement at Benkulen, on the south-west coast near the important pepper-collecting area of Silebar. Despite Dutch attempts to intimidate the local Rajas under cover of suzerainty claims by their client Sultan of Bantam, pepper began to come in – the ship *Williamson* loaded 500,000 lbs/226,800 kgs of the spice in October 1689. After an eighty year history of broken promises to local rulers in Indonesia, the English had finally come to stay. Benkulen, supplemented by supplies from Malabar and later from

Madras, remained a major source of pepper throughout the eighteenth century, regularly sending between 1,000,000 and 2,000,000 lbs/453,600 and 907,200 kgs per year to London. In 1825 the settlement was handed over to Dutch control in exchange for Malacca.

By the end of the seventeenth century the balance between the two Companies began to shift. It was the English, under their new Dutch king, William III, who were more enterprising, aggressive and self-confident, while Holland's real position as a small country facing competition on all fronts from much larger neighbours was becoming apparent. The reasons for the 'decline' of the VOC have been much debated and have been variously attributed to the corruption of its servants, the growing conservatism of its Directors, and the loss of its edge in shipbuilding. Following the catastrophic effects on Dutch seaborne trade of the 4th Anglo–Dutch War of 1780–84 and then the French Revolutionary invasion of the Netherlands, the VOC was dissolved on 31 December 1795. Certainly with hindsight its concentration on Indonesia and its Batavia headquarters proved to be a mistake. Wealth and power lay elsewhere in Asia, as the English were soon to discover.

Bugis sailing ships in harbour at Jakarta (Batavia).

Photograph by the author

India and Textiles

Although the English arrived at Surat in 1608, it was several years before a permanent factory was established. The long presence of the Portuguese on the west coast of India, pre-dating Mughal control, made unhampered access for other Europeans more problematical than on the east or 'Coromandel' coast or at the open port of Bantam.

Surat, the outlet for the textile manufactures of Gujarat and the embarkation point for the annual Haj pilgrimage, was the most important centre for the overseas trade of the Mughal Empire. As well as providing textiles to be exchanged for pepper and spices in Southeast Asia it offered the possibility of participating in and imitating existing trade networks westwards to Persia, a source of raw silk, and into the Red Sea, where Egyptian and Turkish merchants made annual purchases of Gujarati textiles with silver. Surat was also, of course, the first major Asian port city within reach of ships rounding the Cape of Good Hope.

Existing arrangements between the Mughal local authorities and the Portuguese, who held a string of fortified bases along the coast north from Goa backed up by regular naval patrols, were not to be easily overturned. The English had to demonstrate that they could be even more of a menace at sea and that they were capable of defeating Portuguese attacks. This they proceeded to do over the next few years. Sir Henry Middleton plundered the Red Sea shipping in the summer of 1612 and Portuguese fleets were beaten off with great loss, within sight of Surat, in December 1612 and January 1615. Even so, the Mughal authorities would not finally admit the English without Imperial permission, which lead to a remarkable series of early contacts with the Mughal court.

A painted and resist-dyed chintz coverlet from Coromandel, early eighteenth century.

Victoria & Albert Museum: IS.46–1956

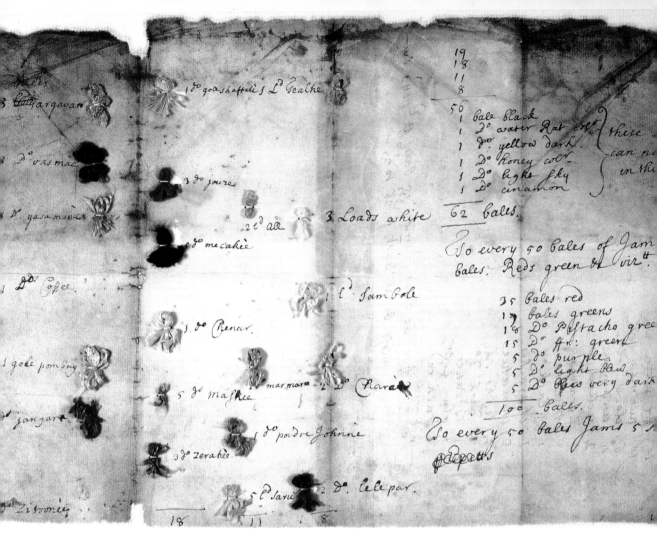

Samples of silk thread available in Persia, 3 August 1697.

British Library, OIOC: G/29/1, f.233

Babur, a Turkic adventurer who claimed descent from the Mongol conqueror Timur or Tamerlane and who had gained control over Afghanistan, invaded India in the mid-1520s. At his death in 1530 the new arrivals had established a loosely-knit empire extending from Kabul to the borders of Bengal. Although they called themselves Mughal, or Mongol, the first generations spoke Turkish. Their successors adopted the Persian language and culture to create perhaps the world's most civilised centre of power, albeit ruthless, filled with all the magnificence and luxury that Asia could supply.

Babur's grandson Akbar, who occupied the throne from 1556 to 1605, consolidated Mughal rule over the whole of northern India, taking in Sind, Kashmir, Gujarat, Rajasthan, Orissa and Bengal, forming a partnership with the Hindu Rajputs to govern through a centralised bureaucracy with officers of state and provincial authorities under his personal direction. More open-minded than most contemporaries, Akbar married a Rajput princess, invited Jesuits, Brahmins, Jains and Zoroastrians to religious discussions, and abolished the poll-tax which had customarily been levied on non-Muslims. Throughout his life he had a love of painting, maintaining artists at his court who produced illustrated manuscripts of Persian classics, Indian texts, histories, biographies, portraits and, to satisfy his curiosity about the outside world, copies of European prints and depictions of European manners and costumes. Akbar's son Jahangir (r.1605–1627) continued the tradition of artistic patronage, priding himself as a connoisseur of painting and thereby offering a fascinating opening for the first English diplomatic exchanges.

The Delhi Gate of the Red Fort at Agra, by an Indian artist, early nineteenth century.
British Library, OIOC: Add.22716

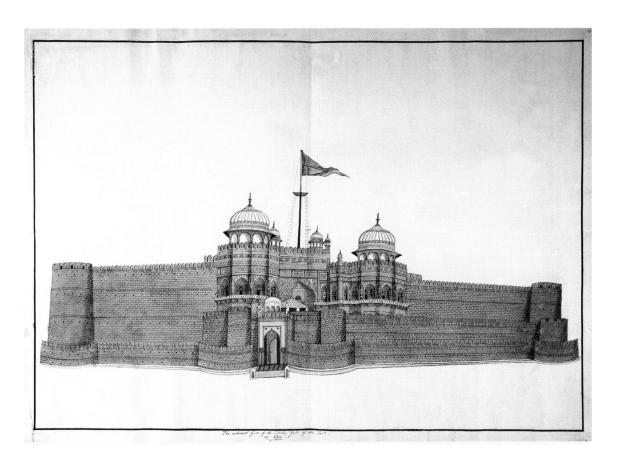

William Hawkins, commander of the *Hector*, left the ship at Surat in 1608 and travelled up to Agra to seek permission for a permanent trade. Even though he had nothing to offer as presents except broadcloth, he made a favourable impression on Jahangir, not least because he could speak Turkish and could match the Emperor's consumption of wine. Pressed to remain, he was made a Captain of 400 horse, he married an Armenian Christian girl chosen by Jahangir and, dressed as a Muslim nobleman, he took his place among the courtiers. Despite such personal standing, a grant of trading privileges was not forthcoming, so he and his wife left Agra for Surat at the end of 1611, getting on board Middleton's fleet in January 1612. He died before reaching England. His widow remarried Gabriel Towerson (who was executed at Amboina in 1623), returned to India with him, and then elected to remain there among her relatives rather than sail for Bantam. Her subsequent fate is not recorded.

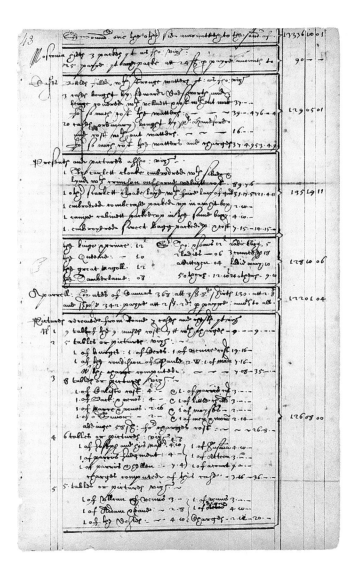

While the Company's Directors issued strict injunctions against
anyone following Hawkins's example, reports of Jahangir's artistic
tastes now caused them to address the question "What do you give to an
Emperor?". The fleet of 1614 carried out 78 oil paintings; 41 of them,
commissioned in London, were portraits of the King, the Queen, Sir
Thomas Smythe, assorted lords, ladies and citizens, and two fanciful
depictions of the 'Great Magoll' and 'Tamberlaine'; the rest, bought
from studios in Rouen, depicted classical and religious subjects like
Mars and Venus, the Judgement of Paris, and Adam and Eve, offering

A section from a panoramic scroll of the city of Delhi viewed from the Lahore Gate of the Red Fort, by Mazhar 'Ali Khan, 1846.

British Library, OIOC: Add.Or.4126

ample opportunity to portray fair and beautiful women. Such novelties were gracefully received but failed to secure permission for an English factory. This had to await the arrival of a 'proper' ambassador in 1615.

Influenced by the unanimous opinion of its servants on the spot that mere merchants had little status at the Mughal court, the Company's Directors persuaded King James I to depatch a special representative at their expense. The man selected, Sir Thomas Roe, was an established courtier, a close friend of Prince Henry (until his death in 1612) and the Princess Elizabeth. Roe remained in India for almost three years. His diary (which is in the British Library's collections) describes the magnificence and intrigues of Jahangir's court. Roe had plenty of experience of courts and their conspicuous consumption, but the apex of the enormous human and natural resources of the Mughal Empire was another world.

At Ajmer in March 1611 Roe was received in audience by Jahangir. The Mughal, wearing pure white clothing 'adorned with more jewels than any other monarch in the world', was seated on a throne raised four feet above the floor, in a hall canopied with hangings of cloth of gold, silk and velvet, with rich Persian carpets underfoot, and with seven of the 1614 oil paintings (including the portraits of the King, the Queen and Sir Thomas Smythe) arranged behind him. It is hard to imagine the other great Asian empire, Ming China, granting such an honour to a 'red-haired barbarian'. The outcome of the embassy was not some formal treaty of commerce between the two rulers, a totally alien concept which Roe soon had to forget. Instead he received an Imperial edict or *farman* assuring good usage of the English, together with a *farman* from Prince Khurram, the new Viceroy of Gujarat (who succeeded as Shah Jahan in 1628), granting favourable conditions of trade at Surat.

A section from a panoramic scroll of the city of Lahore, by an Indian artist, mid-nineteenth century.

British Library, OIOC: Or.11186

The Portuguese position in India had been weakened, though there was serious fighting still to come. From Surat the English began to participate in the Red Sea and Persian trades as well as sending cargoes of textiles to Bantam. In 1617 Shah Abbas of Persia granted a *farman* for English trade at Isfahan and the Gulf port of Jask. In 1619 a new commodity, coffee, was bought at Mokha for sale in Persia. In 1622 the English Company's ships helped the Persians to capture the fortress of Hormuz, the key to the Gulf, receiving as their reward an annual share of the customs revenue of Bandar Abbas, to where the trade was now transferred.

On the other side of India the 1611 settlement at the Golconda port of Masulipatam on the Coromandel coast had maintained a fairly flourishing textile trade to Bantam. In 1639 an invitation to settle from the *naik* or local Hindu ruler of the coastal districts around the small town of Madraspatam, far to the south, was eagerly accepted by the English Company. As well as granting territory and trading rights, the *naik* also licensed the construction of a fortress. Fort St George at Madras was the first of its kind for the English Company, comparable to the earlier Portuguese bases and to the VOC's efforts further east. It was followed by the castle at Bombay, an island commanding a superb harbour 160 miles south of Surat, ceded to the Portuguese by the Sultan of Gujarat in 1534. In 1661 it was transferred to King Charles II as part of the dowry of his Portuguese bride, Catherine of Braganza. He in turn handed it over to the Company, who made it their headquarters for India in 1674. From the 1650s the English had also begun trading in Bengal under a *farman* from Shah Jahan, eventually settling their main factory at the village of Sutanati on the river Hugli, which became the city of Calcutta. Permission to fortify was granted by the Mughal Nawab of Bengal in 1696 and Fort William was completed in 1702. At the turn of the eighteenth century the English presence in India consisted of a sprinkling of small factories along the west and east coasts and inland as far as Patna, plus these three strong points at Bombay, Madras and Calcutta. All owed their existence to Indian permission, partnership and complicity in the business of making money.

Fort William, Calcutta, by
George Lambert and Samuel
Scott, c.1730. The painting is
one of a set of six views (the
others are Bombay, Madras,
Tellicherry, Cape of Good
Hope and St Helena) commissioned by the Company for
the Court of Directors' room
at East India House in
London.

British Library, OIOC: F45

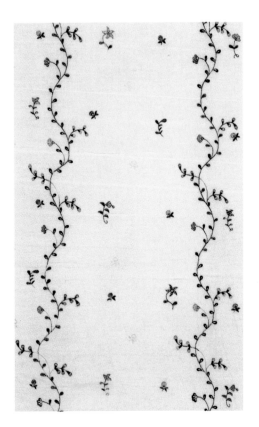

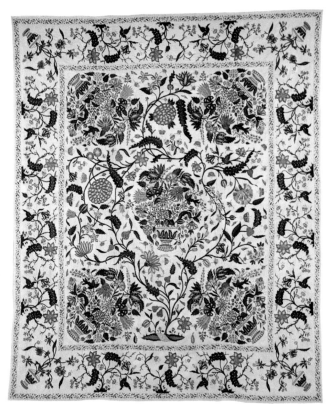

What of the textiles which had driven all this effort to the main
production centres of Coromandel, Gujarat and later Bengal? The
ready availablity of raw cotton, silk and dyestuffs in all three areas had
stimulated, over centuries, the growth of a village-based hand-loom
industry which gave employment to hundreds of thousands of highly
skilled weavers, dyers and washers, producing enormous quantities of
different kinds of cloth for specific market requirements throughout
Asia. A definitive glossary of types has yet to be compiled. Among the
more familiar are fine muslins, painted or printed chintz and palam-
pores, plain white baftas, diapers and dungarees, striped allejaes, mixed
cotton and silk ginghams, and embroidered quilts. Some cloths were
patterned in the loom, others had gold or silver threads woven into
them, but the supreme Indian achievements lay in the mastery of
colour-fast dyeing techniques and the fabulous designs and colour
combinations produced by hand-painting and wood-blocking. The

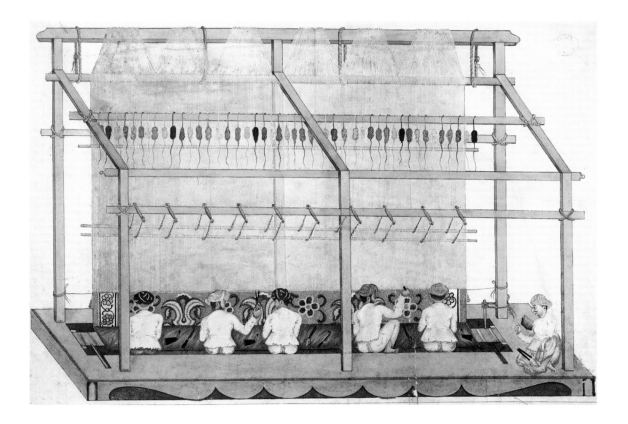

English traders always referred to them as 'piece goods' – each piece was usually about a yard wide (the width of the loom) and between ten and twenty yards long depending upon type.

Originally intended to facilitate the purchase of pepper and spices in Indonesia, once the first cargoes of cloth reached England demand at home grew rapidly – as early as 1620 50,000 pieces of painted and printed chintz were brought in, while as late as the 1750s Indian textiles acounted for 60% of the total value of the Company's sales in London. A typical eighteenth-century order, to Bengal for the season 1730/1, called for 589,900 pieces of 38 different types, sub-divided into 98 varieties.

Procurement of such quantities followed long-established practice. The English factors engaged Indian brokers who were paid a fixed percentage to negotiate and manage contracts with local authorities, village headmen and weaver families for the delivery of stated

OPPOSITE Portrait of a lady, by the Mughal artist Muhammad Afzal, c.1740.
British Library, OIOC: Johnson 11.2

ABOVE A carpet loom at Hunsur in Mysore, by a South Indian artist, 1850.
British Library, OIOC: Add.Or.755

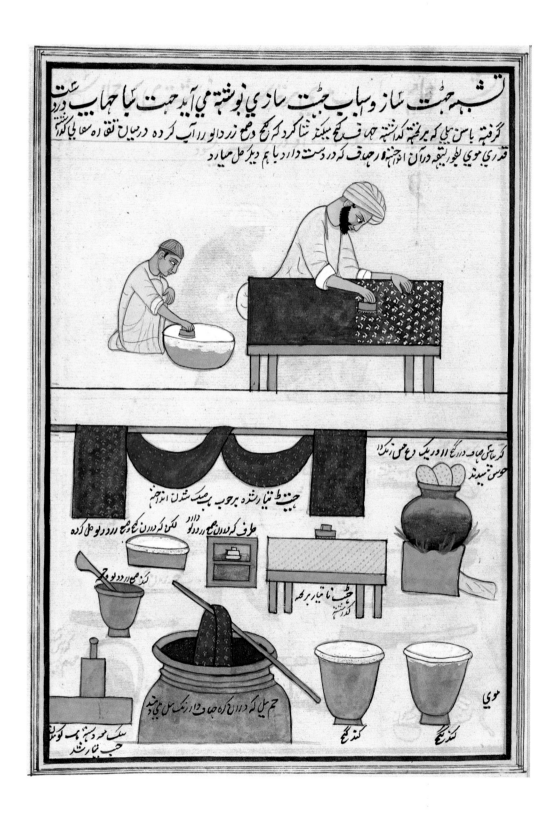

numbers of particular types by specified dates, and who guaranteed the safety of cash advances made by the Company for the purchase of yarn and dyestuffs. The weavers, the ancillary craftsmen and the cultivators of the raw materials were at the bottom of the chain. Frequently devastated by climate, famine and war, they were always subject to varying degrees of pressure and exploitation while the landholders, the brokers and the Company grew rich on their skills.

OPPOSITE A cloth printer, using a hand-block, and a dyer, by a Kashmiri artist, c.1850–60.
British Library, OIOC: Ad.Or.1714

ABOVE LEFT List of Bengal piece goods to be provided for the 1730/1 season.
British Library, OIOC: E/3/5, f.97

ABOVE RIGHT Counterpart of a Company order, written in Bengali, for 4,750 pieces of cloth.
British Library, OIOC: Ben.Ms.4049, f.3

Factors and Factories

Unlike the VOC, which centralised its Asian operations at Batavia, the English Company evolved a fairly loose management structure for its factories. The main centres of Bantam, Surat/Bombay, Madras and later Calcutta were each headed by a President or Governor (though Bantam was reduced to Agency status as Indian textiles took over from pepper and spices in commercial importance), and assisted by a Council of between three and six experienced employees. Each Presidency was responsible for a varying number of subordinate factories directed by Agents or Chiefs, depending on their size. The western India Presidency at Surat/Bombay was recognised as the senior establishment until the early eighteenth century, when Calcutta took over that position.

In a world where long-distance communication was only as fast as the speed of a sailing ship, the Company Directors in London faced two problems – how to take and manage business decisions, and how to keep their servants on the spot industrious, sober and honest. The first was perhaps less of a problem than the second. All business at all stages was carried on in writing, which gives us the term 'writer' for the most junior grade of overseas servant. The result survives today as the massive East India Company archive, deposited in the British Library's Oriental & India Office Collections. 'General' letters exchanged between London and the Presidencies laid down and responded to the Directors' decisions, which were based upon copies of all correspondence between the Presidencies and their subordinate factories, annual returns of all accounts, copies of the minutes or 'consultations' of the meetings of all the Presidency and factory councils, and the ships' journals or logs of all voyages from London. Millions of pieces of paper gradually

OPPOSITE Detail of the Dutch factory at Surat (see page 75).

Neceffaries,

FOR A

WRITER to INDIA,

SOLD BY

WELCH AND STALKER,

(Late EVANS AND WELCH,)

No. 134, LEADENHALL-STREET, LONDON.

A COT. Hair mattrafs and bolfter.	Fowling-piece.
Feather pillow.	Pair of piftols.
Blankets.	Saddle and bridle.
Quilt.	Stationary.
White fheets.	Travelling-cafe.
Pillow-cafes.	Moorifh grammar.
A fet of cot-curtains.	Perfian ditto.
Callico fhirts.	Ditto dictionary.
Night-fhirts.	Ditto interpreter.
White neck-handkerchiefs.	Oufley's Perfian Mifcellanies.
Black filk ftocks.	Carlifle's Arabian Poetry.
Towels.	Razor-cafe complete.
Pocket-handkerchiefs.	Hair-powder and pomatum.
Cotton caps.	Powder bag and puff.
Net-caps.	Boxes of fhaving-powder.
White filk hofe.	Combs and brufh.
White cotton ditto.	Pounds of Windfor foap.
Brown cotton ditto.	Pounds of common foap.
Worfted ditto.	Pewter bafon.
Cotton focks.	Clothes-brufh.
Brown cotton gloves.	Set of fhoe-brufhes and blacking-balls.
White filk ditto.	Silver tea-fpoons and tongs in a cafe.
Mufquetto trowfers.	A mahogany knife-cafe, containing fix
Striped gingum ditto.	large filver fpoons, twelve table knives
Pantaloons.	and forks, and fix defert ditto.
Surtout-coat.	Quart tin mug.
Boat-cloak.	Pint ditto.
Coats of thin cloth.	Tea-kettle or tin boiler.
Fancy-waiftcoats.	Pounds of wax candles.
Cafimere breeches.	Flat candleftick.
Thin waiftcoats with fleeves.	Sciffors.
Thin breeches.	Pen-knives.
Callico drawers.	Cork-fcrews.
Flannel drawers.	Small looking-glafs with flider.
Cloth and trimmings for two coats, to make in India.	Buckles.
	Sleeve-buttons.
Cafimere and trimmings for breeches.	Cafe of inftruments.
Dreffing-gown.	Tin fugar-canifter and padlock.
Foul-clothes bag.	Pounds of lump-fugar.
Needles, thread, &c.	Tea, coffee, and chocolate.
Pieces of hair-riband.	Portable foup.
Pieces of fhoe-riband.	Sage and balm.
Fine hats.	Pounds of tobacco.
Sea-hats.	Folding camp-ftool.
Travelling-cap.	Hamper of wine.
Shoes.	Liquor-cafe.
Boots.	Liquor.
Boot-jack.	Box for books.
Silver-hilted fword.	Trunk.
Silk belt.	Cheft.

'Necessaries for a Writer to India', a handbill issued by a specialist dealer in London, c.1800.

British Library, OIOC: W.7732 (5)

accumulated in London to form the inherited administrative and commercial memory of the Company, the product of never more than two to three hundred personnel actually resident in Asia.

Man management at such distances was always difficult, removed as the Company's employees were from the social constraints of their home environment and facing the ever-present prospect of early death. The Company's main sanction against misbehaviour, apart from peer pressure, was that almost without exception its servants hoped to return home with whatever estate they had managed to accumulate. Appointees were characteristically drawn from the growing urban middle class of merchants and tradesmen. They needed 'connections' because they were required to nominate sureties in England for their good behaviour, who entered into bonds of between £200 and £500 which could be called in as a financial penalty levied against friends and family.

The conditions of factory life were also designed to oversee behaviour. Each factory consisted of a compound containing living quarters, public rooms, warehouses and open yards, the whole surrounded by a fence or wall as security against fire or thieves and, except for Madras, Bombay and Calcutta, none of them were fortified. For instance, the English factory at Hirado in Japan had a wharf fronting the harbour and, as well as the usual buildings, there was a garden with a pond for *koi* carp and a dovecote, an orchard, a vegetable patch, and a Japanese *o-furo* or hot bath, which friends and neighbours were often invited to share. The much grander establishment at Surat, besides 'convenient lodgings to forty persons and decent apartments to the President', had a chapel, a large water reservoir or tank, shaded garden walks, its own *hammam* or Turkish bath, and a library. When it closed in 1682 the Bantam factory had a library of 185 books, mostly religious or classical texts, including a Malay translation of the New Testament, *Jang amyat Evangelia*, published at Oxford in 1677.

Pomp and show were used to establish English status in Asian society, prompting frequent criticisms from the Directors in London. John Fryer, surgeon at Surat in 1674, describes how the President made his visits to the city authorities carried in a palanquin with a horse of state caparisoned in silver led before him, a 'noise of trumpets', a standard-bearer flourishing the flag of St George, a fan of ostrich feathers to keep off the sun, coaches for the gentlemen of the Council, and an escort of forty Muslim cavalrymen.

From the second half of the seventeenth century a handful of seniors who had European wives, usually the relatives of fellow servants, were permitted to live in separate houses outside the factory enclosures, and the small groups of soldiers sent out to garrison the forts at Madras, Bombay and Calcutta were encouraged to marry local women. But most employees lived communally, taking their meals together at the Company's expense and basically spending all their time in each other's company. Apart from their official duties, private trading, drink, sex

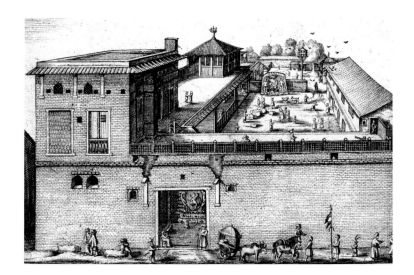

The Dutch factory at Surat, an engraving in Pieter van den Broecke's *Korte Historiael ende Journaelsche Aenteyck-eninghe*, Amsterdam, 1634. Contemporary descriptions make it clear that the English factory had a similar layout.

British Library, 10095.aaa.49

and death formed the background to their collegiate-type life. Drunkenness caused fierce quarrelling, jealousy over private trading produced its own frictions, and there was constant 'whistle-blowing' back to the Directors in London.

Liaisons with Asian women were widespread, whether the casual encounters of seamen visiting the port cities or long-term commitments which could bring a deeper understanding of the local culture. Men who found themselves in isolated subordinate factories seem, however, to have been particularly prone to excess. William Raven, one of only three Englishmen living at the diamond-trading centre of Sukadana in western Borneo, complained to Bantam in 1618 that his chief, George Collins, was a 'great disgrace to Christianity, for in the Company's houses he hath a long time kept four whores which were bought with the Company's money and he hath and doth use all their bodies to fulfill his filthy lust of lechery.' Even worse, 'these not being sufficient for his greedy appetite, he doth also give wages unto other whores which do come into the house daily unto him.' His fate is unknown, but was probably an early death.

It came to be reckoned that while it took five years to acclimatize, most of the Company's servants resident in Asia were lucky to last for two monsoons. Drink, diet and the heat undermined health, while the rainy seasons brought water-borne diseases like cholera and typhoid, followed by malaria. John Ovington, who went out as ship's chaplain on the *Benjamin* in 1689, records that during their stay in Bombay harbour during the monsoon of 1690 twenty out of twenty-four passengers and fifteen of the crew succumbed to various diseases. In some years up to a third of the overseas personnel died, and only a few ever made it back to England as men of means.

Salaries were modest, ranging from £20 a year for a writer and £30 for a factor to £350 or, exceptionally, £500 for a President. Apart from some direct appointments to senior posts, progress was through the ranks, so that promotion came to depend as much on survival as ability. The Company was at first ambivalent about its servants taking advantage of the circumstances in which they found themselves to make money on their own account, even though the prospect of gaining a fortune, however modest, must have been the driving motive for accepting such risky employment. In the first half of the seventeenth century the Directors attempted to suppress all except the most trivial private efforts, especially when they suspected that the Company's money had been 'borrowed'. A typical example is Richard Wickham, who spent five years in Japan on a salary of never more than £55 and yet at his death at Bantam in 1618 left goods and money to the value of £1400. His estate was seized pending investigation.

The compromise that was eventually reached proved to be a significant element in the Company's success. Unlike the VOC, which paid higher salaries while always attempting to root out private trade, the English Company began to concede regulated opportunities for private enterprise. Rules drawn up in 1674 allowed its servants, and the free merchants (mostly ex-employees) who were being permitted to settle at the main factories in India, to trade from port to port within Asia in all but a few commodities which were entirely reserved for the Company. They were also allowed to send to England precious stones, musk, ambergris, certain spices, carpets, and textiles interwoven with gold or silver thread. Ship owners and officers could transport their own goods to and from Asia up to a certain percentage of the ship's tonnage. By the mid-eighteenth century it was estimated that one good voyage as commander of a ship to China, which brought a personal allowance of 38 tons homeward, could set a man up for life.

There were hiccups in the 1670s and 1680s when English ships other than the Company's, known as interlopers, were active in the Indian Ocean. For ten years Ayutthaya in Siam became the free-trading 'Wild West' of Asia under the influence of Constantine Phaulkon, a former Company employee of Greek origin who achieved the position of Siamese Minister for the Affairs of Foreigners. But a combination of fierce reprisals against any Company servants conniving with interlopers, actions in the English courts, a dynastic revolution in Siam during which Phaulkon was beheaded, and the gradual widening of the shareholding membership of the Company in London saw off the problem. The rules were changed regularly, adding new commodities to the lists of Permission and Privilege Goods, or reserving to the Company

الله اكبر

بسم الله الرحمن الرحیم

كسى

جوانب ... سيدي رشيدالدين سلطان
كرمى ... كه دركار قلم

غرض السلام ... به مهرى خلاف مصر خلائق ... علي صحت
مرسدكم

باهم ... مدرسه ... سال سكه كراى دردسته ... كذرحود

مقصود ودرعالم حورى وبادبه ... پوس ... نصرمددآمدكه ... اهلكراى
ربا جكم حصر ... اكبرزادق ندبران سيد حاور كديم حق دراز ... كيسل
وقت دكم ... دلالان ... عوهنرسى ملاك حور حصر عبدہ ... نفيه
پسيار درريم ... دلالان مال فوایل ... ملاك ... هم كرم ... حافظ

سود ... جوده ... جكه كان ... نوسته ... درابنداكى سته ... مالداريم
سطفا ... كرك ... هركدست ... بدازال ... نبرده ... هزارقلعه ... اردشیر
وحبى ... اكبر ... بارسكرده ... وحوامید ... بهدوتل مالكا ... مقررا
راواب ... وماباى ... لامكو ... مقررشا ... مبتدمال ... علم هم
شابه ... كفته ... رقعه ... كرده ... مرى ... معى كردم حوريارد كرد كان
توكراى ... اكبرمرهسند ... محاصر ... دكرمراى فصل حول هردادپاساول

عصه دست ... كه نمودم ... امداد دست كراى هرباكم ... دب جكى جفا
حوزهكرى ... على دست حق مرادان صالح ... جودن اوقاب

لدسراى ... لم ... امى ... جوب

commodities which had previously been allowed. The system was managed by a special Private Trade Committee of the Directors.

For the lucky few private trade could bring great wealth. Elihu Yale, born in Massachusetts in 1648, the son of a Welsh migrant to New England, arrived at Madras as a writer in 1672. A fortunate marriage to the widow of the second most senior member of the Council there brought him the funds to begin speculation in diamonds. Despite a long record of rather shady dealings he served as Governor of Madras from 1687 to 1692, finally returning home in 1699 with a 'prodigious estate', a multi-millionaire by modern standards. He is best remembered today for his gift of textiles and books in 1718 to the newly-founded Connecticut College at New Haven in America. They were sold for nearly £1200 and in honour of his magnificent donation the establishment was renamed Yale College, now Yale University.

Thomas Pitt, son of a Dorset clergyman, was one of the most notorious interlopers of the 1670s and 1680s. He was employed as President at Madras between 1698 and 1709. Equally successful in the Company's business and his own, in 1701 he privately bought a rough diamond of 410 carats from an Indian merchant who had acquired it from an English sea captain who, in turn, had obtained it from a worker in the Golconda mines. The price was £20,000. After cutting and polishing in London, which reduced it to 136½ carats, the stone was sold to the Regent of France for £135,000 and was set into the French crown. Such fabulous profits enabled 'Diamond Pitt' to purchase landed estates throughout England, taking his place as a Member of Parliament and a man of affairs in London. His grandson William was the 'Pitt the Elder' of late eighteenth-century political fame.

Private trade depended on an evolving network of partnerships with members of existing merchant communities throughout Asia. The Company's employees were able to use the contacts arising from their official duties to enter into lucrative arrangements with Asian merchants and ship owners, while the free merchants were in great demand as commanders of ships in what came to be known as the 'country' trade. By the end of the eighteenth century the private enterprise of British 'country' ships, backed up by mainly Indian partners, had come to dominate inter-Asian maritime trade.

OPPOSITE Petition from three Gujarati merchants of Surat to Oliver Cromwell, written in Persian in January 1655, claiming compensation for losses during war with the Dutch.
British Library, OIOC: Reg.16B.XXI, f.27

The Breakthrough to China

The English had come into contact with Chinese merchants, middlemen and migrants throughout Southeast Asia from their earliest days at Bantam, constantly praising them as a nation peculiarly hardworking and sober, though terribly addicted to gambling. The maritime trade of the whole of East Asia, from Japan to Java and Sumatra, was dominated by Chinese junk traffic. The junks came south in search of pepper and other spices, Indian textiles, perfumed woods and tree gums which formed the essential ingredients of incense, and hundreds of natural products which were highly prized in Chinese medicine and gourmet cuisine. They brought silk, silk textiles, porcelain, and economic migrants. Chinese brokers acted as agents in procuring pepper cargoes for the Europeans. They were the retail traders, small manufacturers and spirit distillers of Southeast Asia's port cities. Chinese cultivators grew pepper and opened up new lands for rice and sugar cane. A few held official positions in royal courts from Ayutthaya to Bantam.

The failed venture to Japan between 1612 and 1623 had shattered the Company's idea of selling Chinese silks bought in Southeast Asia in return for Japanese silver. But the dream of direct access to the Chinese mainland, procuring there silks to fuel the inter-Asian trade and selling English manufactures to the teeming millions of the Celestial Empire remained an aspiration of the Company's business schemes.

In the first half of the seventeenth century few of the Chinese goods available at Bantam and other southern ports were imported into England. The VOC adopted porcelain as a cargo for Europe and the fashionable taste for blue and white which is reflected in so many Dutch

Advertising handbill for Edmund Morris of London, repairer of porcelain, c.1770.

British Museum: Banks 37.11

Edmund Morris,
China-Rivetter,
*at the China Jarr, in Grays Inn Passage,
coming into Red Lyon Square Holbourn,*
London.
*Mends all Sorts of China Wares with
a Peculiar Art, which was never before
found out in this Kingdom, so as a Rivetted
Piece of China will do as much Service
as when New; as there are many Impostors
both in Town & Country that make
false Pretentions, I Desire no other
Satisfaction than what the Workman-
ship Merits. NB: if any of my Work
Should come to Pieces, within
Twenty or Thirty Years,—
I will Repair it, without any
Further Expence.*

paintings of the period was soon established. As early as 1623 nearly 64,000 pieces reached Amsterdam, bought from Chinese junks trading at Pattani, Songkhla and Batavia.

The English Company instructed its servants not to meddle with porcelain, though its use was common in the factories and some employees did make individual bargains. For instance, in 1619 Sir Thomas Dale sent home from Batavia a box containing 82 pieces as a present for his brother-in-law. One small development in the 1660s and 1670s was the regular purchase at Bantam of large Chinese jars filled with ginger preserved in sugar syrup – essentially a practical measure as 500 of them were sufficient to ballast a ship.

The problem with direct trade to China was that the Chinese state, unlike the Mughal Empire, refused to allow any Europeans into its ports except the Portuguese at their closely-supervised enclave of Macao. Typically, the VOC soon took the offensive. Two years after their attack on Macao in 1622 the Dutch established themselves near modern Tainan, on the south-west coast of Taiwan, constructing a huge castle which they named Fort Zeelandia. The island, inhabited by aboriginal tribes, was outside Chinese control and had become a seasonal meeting place for Chinese and Japanese trader-pirates.

Cheng Chih-lung, a protégé of Li Tan the 'Captain' of the Chinese trading community in Japan, assisted the Dutch settlement. By the mid-1630s the powerful junk fleet that he built up was their main source of Chinese goods and Chinese immigrants, who began to plant sugar on the island. Fort Zeelandia became the VOC's distribution centre for East Asia, sending porcelain and sugar south to Batavia, and silk, sugar and deerskins north to Japan. The Dutch had been allowed to remain in Japan after the expulsion of the Portuguese, transferring their factory from Hirado to the strictly-guarded artificial islet of Deshima at Nagasaki, from where they pursued an increasingly valuable trade in Japanese copper rather than silver.

In 1644 Manchu invaders from beyond the Great Wall captured Peking and established the Ch'ing dynasty. Cheng Chih-lung's support for the refugee Ming court was continued, after he had surrendered to the Ch'ing, by his half-Japanese son Cheng Ch'eng-kung, immortalised in East Asian historical legend as 'Koxinga', the Dutch version of his Ming title *Kuo-hsing-yeh* or Lord of the Imperial Surname. As the Ch'ing forces swept into southern China, Koxinga held out in the region around Amoy before transferring his fleet to Taiwan in 1661 and driving the Dutch out of the island. He has the rare distinction today of being claimed as a hero by Japan, where Chikamatsu Monzaemon's play 'The battles of Koxinga' is still a feature of traditional theatre, by the People's Republic because he invaded Taiwan, and by the Chinese Nationalists of Taiwan as a symbol of resistance to the mainland.

The English Company now re-entered the East Asian scene. In 1670 Koxinga's son Cheng Ching invited the Bantam factory to open trading relations. The Directors in London were enthusiastic, formulating another elaborate scheme for inter-Asian trade in the region. The theory this time was that English manufactures could be sold in Taiwan for sugar and deerskins which could be exchanged in Japan for copper, which would buy silk textiles in Tonkin (North Vietnam) for Europe and Japan. Taiwan and Tonkin factories were opened in 1672, but the English ship sent to Nagasaki was expelled by the Japanese authorities. The two new factories immediately lost the theoretical basis for their existence, yet both survived.

At Taiwan, operating from the former town hall of the Fort Zeelandia settlement, the English sold pepper and a small amount of broadcloth – scarlet was favoured for the furnishings of Chinese temples – together with large imports of gunpowder, lead, iron and muskets to feed the Cheng war effort. Between 1674 and 1680 Cheng forces held Amoy again. English ships were able to trade in a mainland port for the first time, exporting quantities of silk, porcelain and the new commodity, tea.

Meanwhile, Tonkin was proving to be an excellent source for locally-produced Chinese-style silk textiles, despite serious difficulties in coping with the exactions of the Vietnamese mandarinate, 'who would have the carpet off the table'. Conditions improved slightly when the factory was moved from the Red River delta trading port of Phô Hien to modern Hanoi in 1679. A typical order from London to Tonkin, in 1682, called for 145,000 pieces of various types, including velvets,

The English and Dutch factories on the banks of the Red River at Hanoi, engraved from a drawing by Samuel Baron, 1686.

British Library, OIOC: W.1917

gauzes, plain white peelongs, and lengths patterned in the loom with coloured flowers.

In 1683 Taiwan finally surrendered to the Ch'ing forces, beginning the process which turned the island into a Chinese province. The English were allowed to settle their affairs and were even granted renewed access to Amoy in 1684–85. Now the wars were over the Ch'ing government relaxed the emergency restrictions which it had imposed on overseas trade from the ports of South China. An explosion of junk traffic followed, especially to Batavia. The VOC was able to obtain all the Chinese commodities it required without any urgent need to go to China. The English, who no longer had a southern base after their expulsion from Bantam in 1682, persisted with voyages to the mainland, mounting them from its Indian factories or directly from London. Regular visits were made to Chusan, Amoy and Canton and these were so successful that the Tonkin factory was closed in 1697.

The final breakthrough came at the turn of the century. From 1699 English ships traded at the great city of Canton on the Pearl River almost every year, and from 1715 the Chinese government made Canton the only port for foreign trade. The English were eventually joined there by the merchants of the French, Dutch, Austrian (or Ostend), Danish and Swedish East India Companies, as well as 'country' ships from

India and the Americans after 1784. But for once the English Company was in first and remained the leader of the pack.

Conditions of trade at Canton were very different from India. The Chinese state, while projecting a Confucian disdain for foreign barbarians and their mercantile activities, was well aware that Europeans could be dangerous. It managed to keep them at a distance until the 1830s.

The factories at Canton were built on a strip of land between the city walls and the river front. Europeans were not officially allowed into the city, though they could take recreation on Honan island in the river, and they were only permitted to live in the factories during the annual trading seasons from roughly June to December each year, leaving when their ships sailed. The ships anchored and received cargoes downstream, off the island of Whampoa, where they were required to unload all their guns and powder into Chinese custody. From 1773 the English Company's servants occupied a fine house at Macao during the non-trading months, giving them a permanent presence close to Canton.

Business was controlled, in the taxation interests of the Chinese state, through close cooperation between the Imperial authorities under a Peking-appointed official known as the Hoppo, and a limited number of government-approved wholesalers called the Hong merchants. All orders for and purchases of the main commodities had to be made

The East Indiaman *Rochester* and Chinese junks in harbour at Chusan, drawn in his log by Captain Francis Stanes, 1710.
British Library, OIOC: L/MAR/8/137B, p.150

The factories at Canton – a detail from an 8-metre-long scroll of the Pearl River from Whampoa to the city, painted by a Chinese artist c.1760.

British Library, Map Collection: K.Top.116.23

through members of the Hong Guild, at prices negotiated by them with the up-country suppliers. No single merchant was allowed to provide more than half of any ship's cargo, but small handicrafts like fans, lacquerware and paintings could be bought freely from local shopkeepers. Chinese interpreters handled communications, in Portuguese at first and then in a kind of pidgin which came to be known as 'port lingo' – it was the late eighteenth century before any English mastered the Chinese language, partly because of difficulties in finding any native speaker willing to risk official disapproval by teaching them. Indeed, when the very first British embassy to China reached Peking in 1793, King George III's letter to the Emperor and the latter's reply were written in Latin, a remarkable tribute to the long Jesuit presence at the Imperial court. But demand and profits were such that the trade flourished, whatever the restrictions. Silver flowed into China in unprecedented quantities.

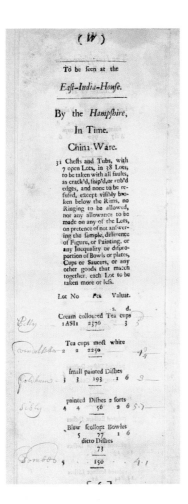

The pre-Canton voyages to ports like Amoy had bought more or less everything on offer, including fans, porcelain figures of animals and deities, Japanese porcelain, cabinets, and wallpaper. At its December 1696 auction in London, the Company even sold one strange lot of costumes for a Chinese opera, which brought £56–11s. Once the regular trade at Canton was established the Company came to concentrate on three principal commodities – tea, silk textiles, and inexpensive porcelain. All the 'fancy' goods and special orders, for example for armorial porcelain or large decorative pieces, were left to the private trade of their servants and ships' officers. Purchases of silk textiles declined during the eighteenth century, although they always formed an important part of the 'country' trade from India.

Extracts from the Company's sale catalogue for March 1704, detailing porcelain imports. British Library, OIOC: H/10 ff.3v, 20v and 24v

14

July — 25 List of Ships Wyndham & Compton's Investment Anno 1733

	Peculs	from	to
Tootenague	1620	T. M. 6:7	T. M. 7:6 ♈ piecul
Tea Bohea	4511	12:8	13:6
Pekoe	171	16:—	21:5
Singloe fine	28		21:—
Bing	165	15:—	23:—
Queen	5		40:—
Powtovan	14		26:—
Conghoe	272		18:—
Hysson 2 sort	122	16:—	25
D° 1st sort	181	25	46

China ware 586 Chests (no Enamell'd)

Sagoe — 154 Peculs

Silks

Ps		from	to
12332 Taffatys		T. M. 4:2	S. M. 4:3 ♈ ps.
2118 Handkercheifs		2:8	3:5
184 Shagreens			4:—
390 Gorgoroons			6:2
700 Sattin			6:7
1200 Goosees			6:—
1800 Poisees (one Colour)			6:7
610 D° (two Colours)			6:7

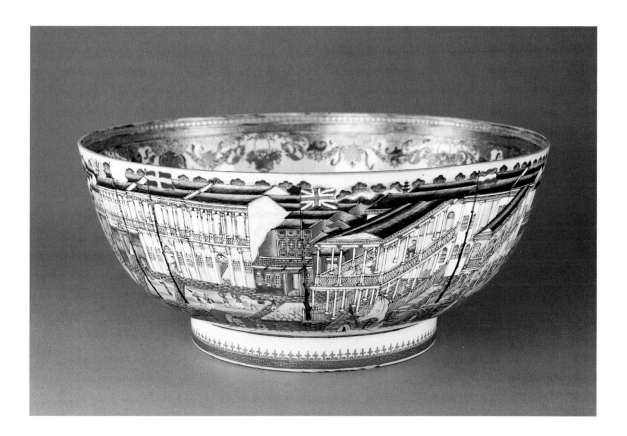

Tea was the new wonder commodity that powered the China trade. Company servants at Bantam and Hirado had become familiar with the universal habit of tea-drinking among East Asian society of all classes, even if the esoterics of the Japanese tea ceremony had eluded them. The tea leaf in all its varieties, infused in boiled water, was recognised by the discerning as a more wholesome daily drink than alcohol. It seems to have been a belief in its health-giving properties, coupled with its exotic novelty status, that launched tea in the West.

On 25 September 1660 Samuel Pepys drank a 'cupp of tee' for the first time. Four years later the Company ordered 'one hundred weight of the best tee procureable' from Bantam, followed by regular orders for small quantities throughout the 1670s. In 1685 the Company's Directors wrote that 'in regard tea is grown to be a commodity here and we have occasion to make presents therein to our great friends at court, we would have you send us yearly five or six canisters of the very best

OPPOSITE List of goods ordered at Canton for the ships *Wyndham* and *Compton*, 25 July 1734.
British Library, OIOC: G/12/36, f.14

ABOVE Punchbowl in coloured enamels with a continuous scene of the factories at Canton, c.1780–90.
British Museum: F.746

OPPOSITE Blue and white plate with a scene of Chinese artisans at work splitting canes, c.1736–50.

British Museum: F.587

ABOVE Pewter box containing six tea caddies painted in coloured enamels, c.1760–1800. The covers are lettered in gold with the names of four black teas – Congo, Gobee (Bohea), Sauchon (Souchong) and Pecko – and two green teas, Heusan (Hyson) and Singlo.

British Museum: F.1688

OVERLEAF Scene in a tea warehouse at the Canton factories, by a Chinese artist, c.1800. The Chinese workers, with their queues tied around their heads, are bringing in the straw containers in which the tea has been transported from the inland growing districts, and emptying them on to a large pile for checking. They are supervised by three Europeans, who are wearing white kerchiefs to protect their hair from the dust, while a fourth is in conversation with a Chinese official. The tea chests, numbered in Western and Chinese scripts, are lined up ready to be filled.

British Library, OIOC: Add.Or.4665

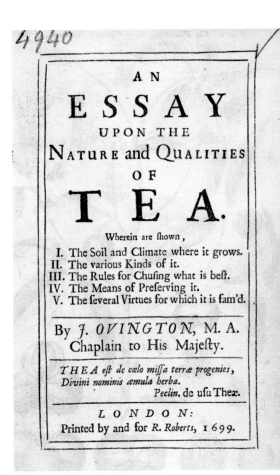

4940

AN
ESSAY
UPON THE
NATURE and QUALITIES
OF
TEA.

Wherein are fhown,

I. The Soil and Climate where it grows.
II. The various Kinds of it.
III. The Rules for Chufing what is beft.
IV. The Means of Preferving it.
V. The feveral Virtues for which it is fam'd.

By *J. OVINGTON*, M. A.
Chaplain to His Majefty.

THEA eft de cælo miffa terræ progenies,
Divini nominis æmula herba.
Peclin. de ufu Theæ.

LONDON:
Printed by and for R. Roberts, 1699.

The GOOD and BAD
EFFECTS
OF
TEA
CONSIDER'D.

Wherein are exhibited,

The Phyfical Virtues of TEA; its general and particular Ufe; to what Conftitutions agreeable; at what Times and Seafons it is moft proper to be drank; and when and how prejudicial.

To which are fubjoined,

Some Confiderations on Afternoon Tea-drinking, and the many fubfequent Evils attending it; with a Perfuafive to the Ufe of our own wholfome Product, SAGE, &c.

By SIMON MASON,
AUTHOR of *The Nature of an Intermitting Fever and Ague confider'd,* lately publifh'd.

Entered according to Act of PARLIAMENT.

LONDON:
Printed for M. COOPER, at the *Globe,* in *Pater-nofter-row.* MDCCXLV.

ABOVE LEFT Title page of John Ovington's 1699 essay on tea. Ovington became an early enthusiast for tea when he was Chaplain at Surat between 1689 and 1693. He recommends it as a remedy against headaches, kidney stones and 'griping in the guts', and suggests that it should be taken with sugar or a piece of preserved lemon.
British Library, 1651/1509

ABOVE RIGHT Simon Mason's 1745 treatise on the good and bad effects of tea is a typical example of the long medical debate over the new drink.
British Library, 1638.l.41

and freshest tea – that which will colour the water in which it is infused most of a greenish complexion is generally best accepted.'

Why tea became Britain's national drink has never been satisfactorily explained. Demand boomed once the Company had access to Canton and by the late eighteenth century tea accounted for more than 60% of its total trade. In 1713 the Company imported 214,000 lbs/97,070 kgs; in 1813 the total was almost 32,000,000 lbs/14,515,200 kgs, and customs duty on tea was providing 10% of the British government's annual revenues. Green varieties predominated at first, but from the 1760s black teas became the more popular. Commercial tea cultivation in India and Ceylon was a late nineteenth-century development. Until then tea meant China.

Along with tea, the Company also began to import massive quanti-

TEAS, &c.

Mesſrs. Morgan and Fenning,

BEG LEAVE TO INFORM

LADIES and GENTLEMEN, having Private Families, that they will be glad to ſupply them with good TEAS, COFFEE, &c. at the undermentioned Prices, for Ready Money only.

BOHEA, CONGOU and SOUCHONG TEAS.

.... Fine Bohea Tea, at per lb. - 2s.
Good Congou Tea, - - - - - 3s.
Ditto, - - - - - - - - - 3s. 6d.
Ditto ditto Breakfaſt Tea, - - 4s.
Fine Congou Tea, for ditto - 5s.
Fine Souchong Tea - - - - 6s.
Fineſt ditto - - - - - - - - 8s.
Superfine ditto - - 9s. to 10s. 6d.

GREEN and HYSON TEAS.

Good Green Tea, - - - - 3s. 4d.
Ditto ditto - - - - - - - 3s. 6d.
Fine ditto - - - - - - - - 4s.
Fineſt Green Tea - - - - - 5s.
Good Hyſon Tea - - - - 5s. 6d.
Fine ditto, Breakfaſt Tea - - 6s.
Fine ditto - - - - - - - - 7s.
Ditto ditto - - - - - - - - 8s.
Fineſt ditto - - - - - - - 10s.
Superfine ditto - - - - - - 12s.
Fine Gunpowder, from 11s. to 14s.

COFFEE.

Good roaſted WEST INDIA COFFEE, from 2s. 6d. to 3s. and 4s.

TURKEY and MOCOA COFFEE, 4s. 6d. to 5s. 6d.

CHOCOLATE, from 3s. 6d. to 5s. 6d.

Sir HANS SLOAN's and CHURCHMAN's Patent Chocolate.

☞ Alſo ſold, MORGAN's GENUINE SAGO POWDER.

*** Letters addreſs'd to them at their Warehouſe, No. 16, *Sherbourne-Lane*, or *New Lloyd's Coffee-Houſe, London*, will be immediately attended to.

N. B. Carriage will be allowed to any Part of *England* or *Wales*, on Quantities exceeding ſix Pounds.

Advertising handbill for Morgan and Fenning of London, tea dealers, 1791.

British Library, 1609/5370

ties of porcelain. In terms of value and share of the total trade it was not of any great significance. It was, however, a useful commodity. Porcelain was cheap, it could be sold for a modest profit, and above all it was an ideal non-polluting cargo to accompany the chests of tea, providing additional ballast for the ships. The versatility of the Chinese craftsmen at the great manufacturing centre of Jingde-zhen near Nanking, long accustomed to the non-Chinese requirements of markets as far away as Constantinople, churned out whatever the customer wanted, in any shape and any pattern.

The Company was not interested in artistic or decorative pieces. Most of its orders to the Hong merchants fell into the two categories of dinner services and sets for tea drinking, either blue and white or in coloured enamels. They were designed for everyday domestic use, hence

Charles Vere

At the Indian King,

The Corner of Salisbury Court, Fleetstreet, N.º 81

London:

Sells all sorts of fine China Ware, the finest Hyson, Congou Teas, Coffee & Chocolate, fine Snuffs, India Tea Tables, with great Variety of India and English Fans, & Fanmounts, and all Sorts of the finest Double Flint Drinking Glasses. The best Goa & Batavia Arrack likewise great Variety of India Pictures, & Rooms hung with the same in the Genteelest Taste & upon the most reasonable Terms.

Wholesale or Retail ..

N.B. Teas and Chinaware for Exportation.

D. 2. 1867

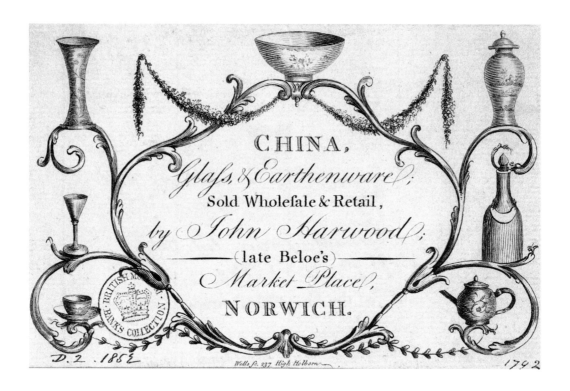

CHINA,
Glass, & Earthenware;
Sold Wholesale & Retail,
by John Harwood;
———(late Beloe's)———
Market Place,
NORWICH.

D.2. 1852   Wells, № 237. High Holborn.   1792

the level of imports. For instance, in 1730 alone the Company brought in over 517,000 pieces, a figure that was maintained throughout the century. Shipwreck salvage during the last twenty years has revealed, in a way that archival statistics never could, the staggering scale of Chinese export production, and the more humdrum pieces have now taken their place alongside the treasured survivors of the private trade.

As developments in India changed the whole nature of the English East India Company's position there, it was the China trade that provided both its continuing commercial justification and the revenues that bolstered its continuing existence.

OPPOSITE Advertising handbill for Charles Vere of London, dealer in tea, porcelain and fancy goods, 1772.

British Museum: Banks 37.24

ABOVE Trade card for Harwood of Norwich, porcelain dealer, 1792.

British Museum: Banks 37.7

From Trade to Empire

The profound changes in the world order which resulted in the subjection of most of Asia to European colonial rule, economic domination, and varying degrees of political interference began in India.

By 1750 the Mughal Empire was in a state of collapse, although emperors in name continued to preside over a court at Delhi and to provide forms of historic legitimacy to events over which they had no control. Shah Jehan's son Aurangzeb (r.1658-1707) had spent the last twenty years of his life fighting off the Hindu Marathas of the western Deccan and the coastal areas south of Bombay. The Maratha bid for national power failed but they remained as powerful and ruthless marauders. A broken and disputed succession eventually brought Muhammad Shah (r.1719–48) to the throne. In the 1720s his chief minister withdrew from Delhi to set himself up as a semi-independent ruler at Hyderabad. In 1738 the Marathas reached the outskirts of Delhi, retiring with the enforced cession of Malwa province, which drove a wedge between the northern and southern halves of the empire. This was followed in 1739 by the great raid of Nadir Shah of Persia, who sacked Delhi and carried off the fabled Peacock Throne and the Koh-i-Noor diamond as part of the plunder. During civil wars after 1748 Sind, Gujarat, Oudh and Bengal broke away from any effective Mughal control.

The emergence of regional states throughout India brought opportunities undreamt of by mere traders as the English Company became a participant in the power politics of the successors to the empire. France, which had established its Compagnie des Indes in 1664 although it was only a serious player from the 1720s, and Britain, extended their European wars to North America, to the Indian Ocean

The Emperor Muhammad Shah seated at a window, by a Mughal artist, c.1720–30.

British Library, OIOC: Add.Or.2769

and to southern India. Between 1744 and 1761, by when the French were defeated, they confronted each other directly at sea and on land and indirectly as allies of rival claimants to the thrones of Arcot and Hyderabad. The Royal Navy became a presence in the Indian Ocean. The Company, initially at Madras, raised its own armies of Indian soldiers.

In 1756 Siraj-ud-Daula, the new young Nawab of Bengal, took the Company's settlement at Calcutta following a refusal to stop strengthening its fortifications against possible French attack. A force from Madras under Robert Clive recaptured the city and at Plassey in June 1757 defeated the Nawab. Mir Jafar, an elderly general, was installed in his place in return for a personal payment to Clive of £234,000. Ambition and greed fuelled episodes of king-making to serve British interests. Mir Jafar was deposed by the Company in 1760 in favour of the supposedly more pliable Mir Kasim, who paid £200,000 to the Bengal Council for the privilege. He turned out to be not so pliable and went to war against the Company in alliance with the Emperor at Delhi and the ruler of Oudh.

The British victory at Buxar in 1764 was followed in 1765 by the Treaty of Allahabad which gave formal Mughal recognition to the Company's assumption of the *diwani* of Bengal. A trading company was now responsible for the civil, judicial and revenue administration of India's richest province, with some twenty million inhabitants. The bleeding of Bengal and the process that created the British Raj had begun. It was backed up by Indian collaboration at all levels and by the ever expanding strength of the Bengal, Madras and Bombay Armies, tens of thousands of volunteer Indian soldiers commanded by a British officer cadre and assisted by regular British Army units posted to India at the Company's expense. The trade continued, but the Company was no longer a supplicant at Indian courts and ports. Over time the whole economic structure of the sub-continent came to serve the needs of the new rulers.

The next seventy years or so have been characterised by recent historians as the 'hybrid' Raj. The Company's servants, transforming themselves from merchants into administrators, judges, revenue collec-

Lt-Col James Skinner
(1778–1841), by William
Melville, c.1836. Skinner, the
son of a Company officer and a
Rajput lady, commanded an
Irregular Cavalry corps of the
Bengal Army, which became
famous as 'Skinner's Horse'.

British Library, OIOC:
851270, f.9

tors and soldiers, eagerly adopted the manners and life-styles of their
Mughal predecessors, played out in the Indian-built stuccoed and clas-
sical-columned Palladian mansions of Calcutta, the 'city of palaces', or
at client courts like Lucknow. Administrative, judicial and revenue
responsibilities demanded a deeper knowledge of both Hindu and
Muslim India. Company servants and army officers became the new
patrons of Indian artists and craftsmen, and the intricacies of Indian
classical and modern languages began to be explored.

Sir William Jones studied Persian in England before going out to
Calcutta as a judge of the Supreme Court in 1783. After founding the
Asiatic Society of Bengal in 1784 he went on to pioneer the study of

خطوبت و دو و داع دارد نانسقه کند از صح عمارت سی دو و داری ست
سرفرازان کند المردوی د اشکل که فردس خرد ازعباس فدداس سان کفهای نجی

براکه دوش کند مکند کورکسی ساندی یازد کازرناب کوین توریسد
امان این نصب نمود بند محلا ازروی زمین فایر کلی لکصد ونعه کنزست

Sanskrit, publishing the first printed book in the language, *The Seasons* by Kalidasa, in 1792. Richard Johnson, a Bengal civil servant from 1769 to 1790, collected manuscripts and Indian miniatures being disposed of by cash-strapped Mughal aristocrats. His collection was sold to the Company's library in London in 1807. The Bengal Army officer William Knox, who represented the Company at the court of Nepal between 1803 and 1805, encountered esoteric Buddhism and had himself depicted receiving a manuscript of the *Lalitavistara*, the most popular Sanskrit biography of the Buddha, from its Nepali scribe. Other individuals commissioned Indian artists to depict the topography, flora and fauna of India, bringing about the fusion of styles which is now called 'Company' painting.

Relations between the new rulers and the ruled seem to have been largely based upon class rather than race. Separation and racist exclusivity came in the nineteenth century. But just as the nature of society at home began to change and England turned into Britain, so too did

OPPOSITE European sight-seers visiting the Taj Mahal at Agra, by a Mughal artist, mid-eighteenth century.
British Library, OIOC: Or.2157, f.611v

ABOVE Ghazi-ud-din Haidar, Nawab of Oudh, entertaining Governor-General Lord Moira and his wife to a banquet in the palace at Lucknow in October 1814, painted by a court artist.
British Library, OIOC: Add.Or.1815

the make-up of the Company's personnel, especially in India. Scots and Protestant Irish provided increasing numbers to the civil and military cadres (the Welsh had long found themselves subsumed within Englishness), and Catholic Irish enlisted men began to be a major element in the European regiments of the Company's armies, making their own contribution to a growing Eurasian community. Evangelical Christianity, present among the Company's Directors and gradually permeating their overseas appointments, hastened the evolution of a sense of 'special mission' and 'imperial duty' as the British became the paramount power in India.

There were two significant developments elsewhere in Asia. After the French Revolutionary armies occupied Holland, Company forces from India invaded Dutch Ceylon in 1796 and in 1811 took Java. Thomas Raffles, a Company man who served as Governor of Java until 1815, went on to found a new settlement at Singapore in 1819 with the agreement of the Sultan of Johore. His vision of an international free-trade emporium at the junction of the Indian Ocean and the China Seas, driven by the entrepreneurship of the British 'country' trade from India and the industriousness of overseas Chinese settlers harked back to the great days of the Sultanate of Malacca and proved a remarkable portent for the future.

Meanwhile the trade to China had begun to fall victim to a vicious traffic in opium, without precedent before the modern outpourings of opium derivatives from Afghanistan and the Burma-Thailand-Laos Golden Triangle, and of cocaine from Colombia. Opium had long been in use throughout Asia as a valued medicine which could deaden pain, assist sleep and reduce stress, while carrying with it the risk of rapid addiction and physical debilitation. China in particular developed a taste for the drug, so much so that as early as 1729 an Imperial edict prohibited its sale.

The Company's purchases at Canton were made almost entirely in bullion. The search for a commodity which the Chinese would accept instead of at least part of the silver focused at first, with reasonable success, on raw cotton from western India, carried by the 'country' traders as well as Company shipping. The takeover of Bengal opened

OPPOSITE ABOVE AND BELOW Captain William Knox, who commissioned this Sanskrit manuscript of the *Lalitavistara* or Sutra of Great Magnificence, is shown receiving it from the scribe Amrtananda in a miniature and on the inside of the back cover. Nepal, 1803. British Library, OIOC: Ms.San.688

up a new possibility. Mughal revenue-raising practices had routinely included state monoplies on the production and distribution of certain commodities. Following this example, in 1773 the Company assumed the monopoly of opium growing in Bengal.

The drug was sold at public auction in Calcutta and soon began to be smuggled into China in ever increasing quantities. Company ships were strictly forbidden to carry opium, thus avoiding difficulties with the Canton authorities. It was carried instead by 'country' traders and a new breed of ruthless agency houses, who offloaded the opium at the regular rendezvous island of Lintin in the mouth of the Pearl River estuary. Corrupted Chinese bureaucrats and customs officials connived at the trade, but no more so than the Company. The hard cash received from the sale of opium to Chinese drug-runners at Lintin was paid into the Company's factory at Canton in return for bills of exchange drawn on London or Calcutta, so 'laundering' the proceeds and providing the Company with an immediate supply of silver for its legitimate purchases.

Opium production at the Company's Patna factory soared, 'country' traders began to bring in further supplies from Malwa in western India, outside Company control, and other Europeans and the Americans bought supplies in Turkey. By 1825 opium imports had over-taken raw cotton and much of the silver that was needed to buy the Company's tea was no longer being carried to China, it was coming from within China. The raw opium was shipped in chests containing about forty large balls each. In 1828–29 alone 12,665 chests reached China.

Free trade in East Asia came to mean the lucrative and immoral freedom to deliver drug cargoes to Chinese addicts. The Chinese state's belated attempt to interrupt the traffic resulted in war in 1840, humili-ating defeat, and the British seizure of Hong Kong island. Victorian values of the later nineteenth century had little effect on Indian opium production, which was contributing more than £9 million a year to Indian government revenues in the 1870s. By then the drug was in world-wide use as the main ingredient of a host of patent medicines based on the alcohol-opium mixture known as laudanum.

Scenes in the Patna opium factory, from the London weekly magazine *The Graphic*, 24 June 1882.

British Library, Newspaper Collection

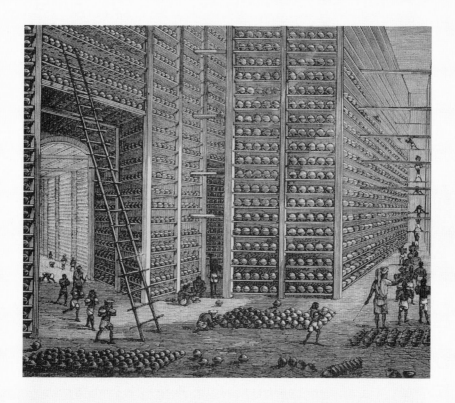

Asia in Britain

The most visible effects of Asian trade on Britain were, or course, the gradual evolution of new consumer tastes and the growth of mass markets for commodities previously unknown.

The pepper and spices which began the trade were nothing new, the English East India Company's activities simply made them more widely available and affordable. It was Indian textiles that had the first major impact. Their wonderful workmanship, colour-fastness and comparative cheapness ensured their rapid success, and by the second half of the seventeenth century they were the most valuable part of the Company's trade into London. Chintz, muslins and innumerable other varieties were seized upon for clothing of all kinds, bed covers, hangings, curtains and other house furnishings.

Welcomed initially as an alternative to linen imports from mainland Europe, the formidable competition they offered both to traditional woollen manufactures and to England's growing silk-weaving industry caused serious agitation in the 1690s. The Company's raw silk imports from Persia and elsewhere had fed the looms of Huguenot refugees from France who settled mainly in the Spitalfields area of London and at Canterbury. The arrival of Chinese-type silk textiles from Tonkin and then mainland China was seen as such a threat that rioting weavers attacked East India House in January 1697. Polemic pamphlets with titles like *England and India inconsistent in their manufactures* or *The English winding sheet for the East India manufactures* fuelled an expanding debate, while an alliance of weavers, dyers, linen-drapers and commercial rivals produced an Act of Parliament in 1700 prohibiting the use and wearing of Asian textiles. The Company's immediate response was to concentrate upon re-export,

The old East India House, Leadenhall Street, London, by George Vertue, c.1711.

British Library, OIOC: WD.1341

but protectionist legislation had little effect against market forces and the popularity of Asian textiles continued throughout the eighteenth century.

Coffee was the next commodity to sweep the country. The drink, with its associated world of the coffee-house, had been encountered by traders to the Levant. The first coffee-house in London was opened in 1657 by a merchant retired from the Smyrna trade. Within six years there were 83, rising to almost 500 in London alone by the early 1700s. Coffee-houses became important venues for exclusively male social and business intercourse, in rooms full of tobacco smoke where newspapers and pamphlets were freely available. Different establishments evolved their own particular styles and clienteles. Deals were struck, businesses were founded and political groupings were forged in the ambience of the coffee-house. But coffee, which was brought in by the Company from Mokha in the Yemen, was soon overtaken by the craze for tea and the Company's cargoes were largely re-exported to coffee-drinking northern Europe.

Tea began as an exotic fashion among the elite which spread through the whole of Britain. By the late eighteenth century it had become the universal daily drink of even the poorest industrial and agricultural workers, taken black and strong, with milk, and cheap sugar from the West Indies. The leisured classes evolved their own essentially feminine and domestic version of the 'tea ceremony', accompanied by the new imports of Chinese porcelain – teapots, cups and saucers, sugar bowls, milk jugs, slop dishes and dainty plates for sugar and spice confections.

The growing wealth generated by the Company also had an economic and physical impact on London, the largest city in Europe by 1700. The diffused profits of the trade played their part in its great series of speculative-built expansions westwards into the elegant squares and terraces successively of Covent Garden, Soho, St James's, Bloomsbury, Mayfair and St Marylebone, where the products of Asia became the consumer staples of upper and middle class life and shopping emerged as a leisure activity. The Company's trade was a major generator of employment in London. Its massive warehouses

OPPOSITE TOP Front elevation of the East India Company's new warehouses in Fenchurch Street, London, 1806.
British Library, OIOC: H/763B, f.7

OPPOSITE BOTTOM East India House, Leadenhall Street, London, by Thomas Hosmer Shepherd, c.1825. The old wooden house was rebuilt between 1726 and 1729 to the designs of Theodore Jacobsen. His building was enlarged in 1753–54 and was then replaced between 1796 and 1799 by this magnificent new headquarters, designed by Richard Jupp.
British Library, OIOC: WD.2881

OVERLEAF 'A view of the East India Docks', by William Daniell, 1808. The view is taken looking south to the Greenwich peninsula, with the sweep of the river around the Isle of Dogs at the right.
British Library, OIOC: P838

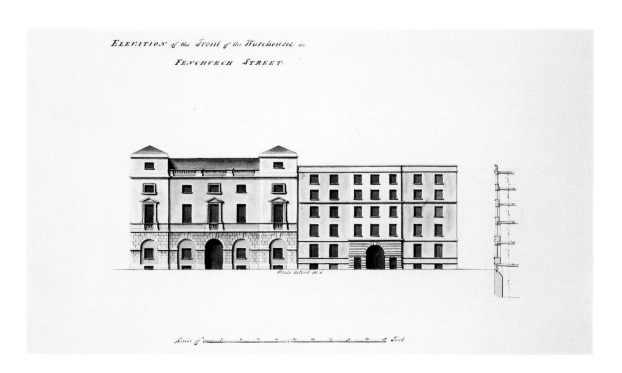

ELEVATION of the Front of the Warehouses, in FENCHURCH STREET.

The Directors' Court Room at East India House, by Thomas Hosmer Shepherd, c.1820. The paintings and furniture survive among the Oriental & India Office Collections at the British Library, while the coat of arms now hangs in the Library's OIOC Reading Room.

British Library, OIOC: WD.2465

loomed over the eastern side of the city. Its old wooden headquarters in Leadenhall Street was transformed into a great commercial mansion. Shipbuilding for the trade, with seamen to man the ships, involved thousands along the river, and between 1803 and 1806 the ship owners built the East India Docks at Blackwall.

The Company had always needed friends at court and in Parliament, not least to fight off challenges to its monopoly of trade to Asia. Opposition in the late seventeenth century which even saw the sanctioning of a rival 'New Company' in 1698 was seen off by a negotiated merger in 1709, coupled with an expansion of the shareholding membership. Serious objections to the Company's activities re-emerged after the takeover of Bengal. Society at home was accustomed to embracing the self-made man, returning from distant parts of the world to set himself up with a country estate, a town house and perhaps a seat in Parliament – it could even accomodate the occasional millionaire. But the new 'nabobs' of the Company's service were returning with

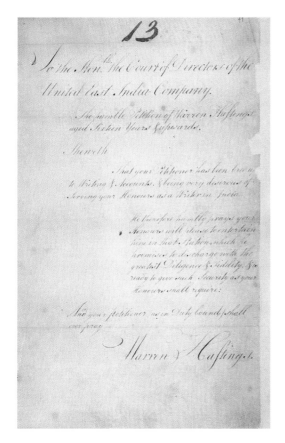

fortunes equalling those of the landed aristocracy without, it would appear, either too much effort or ability. A corrupt political system at Westminster combined jealousy with morality to curb the corruption of Company rule in India.

The Regulating Act of 1773 introduced changes in the election of the Directors and made Calcutta the seat of government, under a Governor-General in Council. Warren Hastings, the President in post, assumed the new title and responsibilities. Charles James Fox introduced an India Bill in 1783 which would have transferred the entire government and patronage of the Company to a Parliamentary Board of Commissioners for the Affairs of India. After his administration fell, William Pitt's revised act of 1784 limited the Board to revision and control of the Company's political decisions, leaving its trade and patronage untouched. Robert Clive had managed to escape relatively

ABOVE LEFT Petition of Warren Hastings for employment as an East India Company writer in 1749.
British Library, OIOC: J/1/1, f.49

ABOVE RIGHT Warren Hastings, by a Mughal artist, c.1782. The miniature is one of the illustrations in a manuscript of the Persian prose works of Mir Kamar al-Din.
British Library, OIOC: Or.6633, f.67r

The TEMPTATION in the WILDERNESS.

Then Reynard taketh them unto an exceeding high Mountain, and shewed them all the kingdoms of the East and the Glory of them, saying all these will I give ye, if ye will fall down and Worship me.

ABOVE 'The Temptation in the Wilderness', political caricature by James Gillray, 1783. Charles James Fox looks out towards India, with the ruins of East India House behind him.

British Library, OIOC: P1776

RIGHT Admission ticket for the trial of Warren Hastings in Westminster Hall, 1788.

British Library, OIOC: Mss Eur B.254

OPPOSITE 'A Transfer of East India Stock', political caricature by James Sayer, 1783. Charles James Fox carries off East India House into a stronghold of the Crown.

British Library, OIOC: P1792

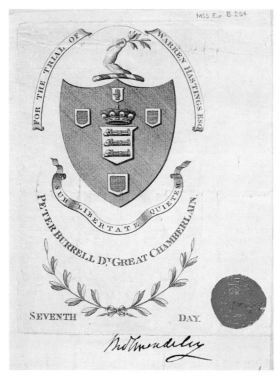

unscathed. It was Warren Hastings who was called to answer to the new morality. Returning to England in 1785, he was impeached on charges of mismanagement in a spectacular show trial at Westminster. The spectacle and the excitement gradually faded as the trial dragged on from 1788 to 1795, when he was finally acquitted.

In 1813 the Company's monopoly of Asian trade was limited to China. The China monopoly was abolished in 1833. After 231 years the Company's trading days were over, yet it lingered on as the proxy administrator of British rule in Asia. The shattering revolt of its Bengal Army in 1857 was followed by final abolition in 1858 and the British Crown assumed the mantle of a British Raj.

Where did Asians themselves feature on the British scene? The answer is, intermittently and in very small numbers. David Middleton brought a Javanese boy back with him in 1611, but his fate is unknown. Eleven Japanese seamen were hired by John Saris for the homeward voyage of the *Clove* in 1614. Surviving a London winter with the help of warm clothing provided by the Directors, they reached Hirado again in August 1617 and immediately began to dispute their wages. In 1626–27 Nakd Ali Beg, ambassador from Shah Abbas of Persia, was received by King Charles I. The Directors commissioned the artist Richard Greenbury to paint two portraits, giving him one as a memento, along with two barrels of wine for his homeward voyage on a Company ship. The other survives among the British Library's Oriental & India Office Collections.

In April 1682 two ambassadors from the 'old' Sultan of Bantam arrived in London, seeking cannon and gunpowder for an imminent civil war. Engraved depictions of Kyai Ngabehi Naya Wipraya and Kyai Ngabehi Jaya Sedana circulated as popular broadsheets. They had royal audiences at Windsor and Whitehall, lavish entertainment at East India House, and were taken to see the sights of the city. John Evelyn thought that they constantly chewed betel 'to preserve them from the toothache, much raging in their country'. What they thought of a performance of Shakespeare's *The Tempest* is not recorded.

The seventeenth-century documents actually have far more references to 'strange beasts' from Asia than to people. Monkeys, exotic deer, parrots, mynah birds and waterfowl were brought in by enterprising Company servants and seamen for the royal menagerie at the Tower of London or for sale to collectors of curiosities. William Methwold, returning from Surat in 1639, carried a supposedly tame tiger cub on board ship, but after it bit him on the right hand and then severely mauled a seaman it was destroyed. In 1675 a young elephant was accompanied to London by two Bantanese handlers, while in a notable flight of private enterprise the captain of the *Herbert* brought home a rhinoceros from Golconda in August 1684, an animal which had not been seen in Europe since 1515. It was put on exhibition at a London tavern at one shilling a time, or two shillings for those wishing to ride on its back. The poor creature died in 1686.

The Bantam ambassador Kyai Ngabehi Naya Wipraya, engraved from a drawing by John Oliver, 1682.

British Museum, P&D: 1849.3–15.100

During the eighteenth century Company personnel were routinely accompanied from and to India by Indian domestic servants. Numbers are difficult to quantify – the archival sources are largely concerned with ensuring that their passage money was paid by their employers – though a fuller picture might emerge from a detailed examination of the passenger lists entered into thousands of ships' logs. Indian and Chinese seamen, known as lascars, found occasional employment on Company ships, and from the 1790s significant numbers began to appear in London. During the Revolutionary and Napoleonic Wars with France the routine seizure or 'pressing' of Company seamen by Royal Navy ships in Asian waters could only be compensated for by hiring local sailors for the return voyages. For instance, of the 3680 seamen who left London in the ships of the 1813 season, 744 were pressed, to be replaced by 1052 lascars. In London the lascars were lodged, clothed

Author. Printed for Thomas Flesher at the Angel and
Crown in St. Pauls Church-yard.

A Very strange Beast called a Rhinoceros, lately
brought from the East-Indies, being the first that ever
was in England, is daily to be seen at the Bell Savage Inn on
Ludgate-Hill, from Nine a Clock in the Morning till Eight
at Night.

A LL Persons born in the County of Northampton are
desired to take Notice, That there will be held a Coun-

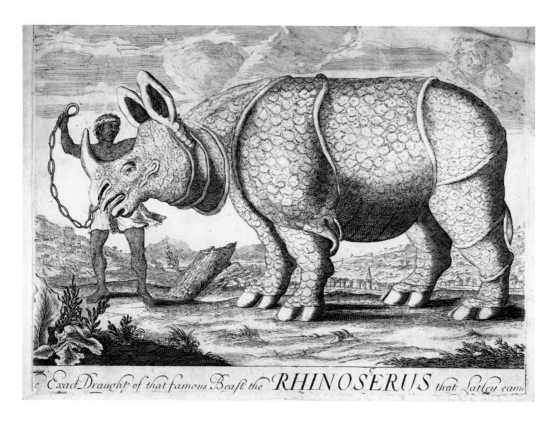

Exact Draught of that famous Beast the RHINOSERUS *that Lately came*

and fed at Company expense in boarding houses close to the river before
returning to Asia as passengers on outward-bound ships. Conditions,
which were often sordid, became the subject of much concern. A few
lascars remained, to form the first of the Asian dockland communities
which eventually grew up in the major ports of Victorian Britain.

Some arrivals were neither servants nor seamen. Mirza I'tisam al-
Din was sent to England in 1765 with a letter to King George III from
the Mughal Emperor Shah Alam. His account of his travels, written in

List of Danish prisoners per Walthamstow

Mr. Stanning Surg.t Mate   Came on board Jan.ry 13
Mr. Termohlen Capt.ns Clerk   at Bangor —
Alexr Dein   Landed in the River
H. Ebbeson   } Boys   in the 11th & 12 July 1
E. I. Jacobson Seaman

List of Lascars per Walthamstow homeward, & Ships Comp.y

Serang	25 Ganlem Hussuin
Mommot	Beehow
Tindals	Ismael
Dane	Abeullah
Ramjou	Canneau run at Madras
Lascars	30 Saccack
Bannou	Fickerou
5 John	Jammael
Hammear	33 Baskatolloh
Cocheal	
Nassib	
Abeullah	I do declare upon honor
10 Dinna	that the above are true &
Esop	correct lists of the Ships
Boro Perou	Comp.y & Passengers to the
Ismael	best of my knowlege &
Chuta Perou	belief. —
15 Sick Mahomed cueat La	
Mamdie	Witness John B Sotheby.
Chutta Abeullah	
Herou	C. Collingwood / Chief Officer.
Haxis	
20 Hammoon	
Mambeccas	
Salomen	

MIRZA ITESA MODEEN.

R.J.Lane del.   C.Bullenandel sculp.

شگرف نامہ ولايت

SHIGURF NAMAH I VELAËT,

OR

Excellent Intelligence concerning Europe;

BEING THE

TRAVELS

OF

MIRZA ITESA MODEEN,

IN

GREAT BRITAIN AND FRANCE.

TRANSLATED FROM THE ORIGINAL PERSIAN MANUSCRIPT INTO
HINDOOSTANEE, WITH AN ENGLISH VERSION AND NOTES,

BY

JAMES EDWARD ALEXANDER, Esq.,

LIEUT., LATE H.M. 13th LIGHT DRAGOONS,

And Adjutant of the Body Guard of the Honourable the Governor of Fort St. George, &c.
Author of Travels in Ava, Persia, and Turkey.

WITH A PORTRAIT OF THE MIRZA.

LONDON:
PRINTED FOR PARBURY, ALLEN, AND CO.
LEADENHALL STREET.

MDCCCXXVII.

ABOVE Mirza I'tisam al-Din,
and the title page of the
translation of his travels,
London, 1827.

British Library, OIOC:
306.23.A.41

OPPOSITE Din Muhammad,
in the frontispiece to his
Shampooing, published at
Brighton in 1822 and 1826.

British Library, OIOC:
T.12646

Persian, was published in an Urdu and English translation in 1827. Din Muhammad, an Indian officer of the Company's Bengal Army, accompanied his friend Captain Godfrey Baker home to Cork in 1784, where he married a local girl and published in 1794 the first book written in English by an Indian, *The travels of Dean Mahomet*. Moving to London with his wife and family around 1807, in 1810 he opened the

S.D. Mahomed,
Shampooing Surgeon,
BRIGHTON.

Published June 1822, by J. Cordwell, at his Repository, 20, Great East Street, Brighton.

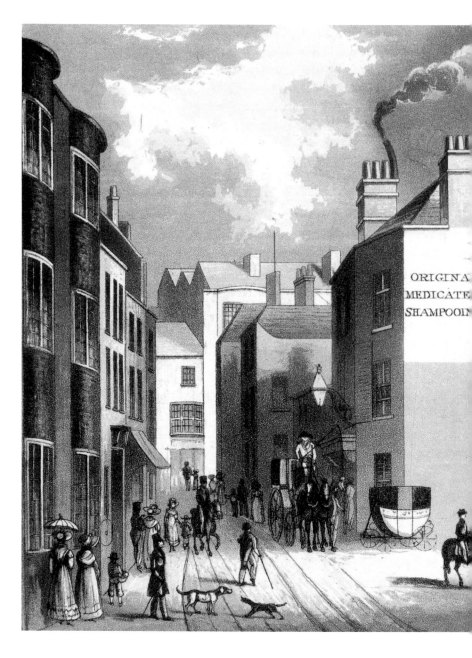

Hindostanee Coffee House at 34 George Street on the fashionable
Portman Estate, offering Indian cuisine in surroundings furnished with
bamboo chairs and oriental landscapes. Surviving bankruptcy in 1812,
he went on to manage a bath-house at Brighton before opening his
own splendid establishment on the seafront, re-inventing himself as a

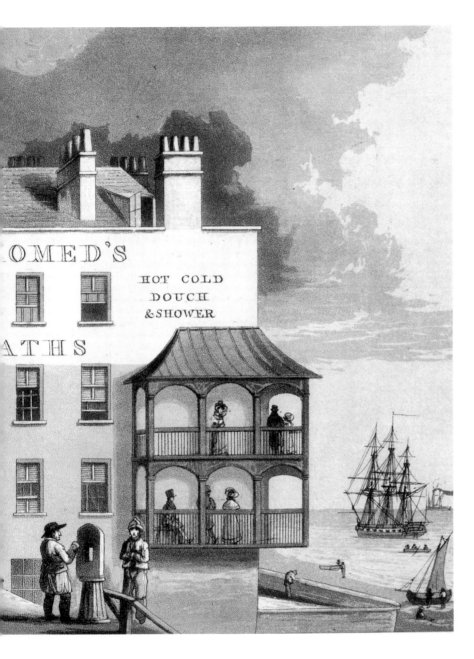

'shampooing surgeon'. He died at Brighton in 1851.

While the products of Asia became an integral part of the British way of life and the politics of the British presence in Asia became the business of the British Parliament, Asians themselves were only rarely encountered in the Company's Britain.

Epilogue

Four hundred years after its first footing in Asia the English East India Company has disappeared from the British consciousness almost without trace. There are a few physical remains in London, like the empty basins of the East India Docks now ringed by skyscrapers, or a massive warehouse block converted to smart offices and loft apartments. Yet the influence of its trade is still all around us, in our tastes, in our language, and in our history.

Maritime trade to Asia proved to be one of the historical forces which created our modern 'globalised' world. It was not the only one of course, for no mention has been made of forces like the European colonising impetus into the Americas or the barbarities of the African slave trade, financed in part by East India-generated capital.

The outcome of European trade became European, especially British, domination of Asia. Few countries escaped direct colonial rule and even fewer the impact of machine industrialisation. Indian textiles gave way to the products of Lancashire mills, even Chinese porcelain was abandoned for the cheaper offerings of Stoke-on-Trent, and the economies of Asian countries were manipulated to turn them into producers of raw materials or food crops and consumers of European, largely British, manufactures. The small niche markets which remained came to resemble the earliest days of the Company's trade in exotic luxuries.

The post-1945 upheaval in Asia, not least the demise of Britain's empire, has seen the emergence of powerful Asian economies once again exporting sophisticated manufactures to the rest of the world. The successors to the Company's trade are perhaps the great industrial-financial complexes to which it gave birth – Bombay, Calcutta, Singapore and Hong Kong – and the now familiar Asian presence in and contribution to a multi-ethnic and multi-cultural Britain.

Further Reading

The most recent, and recommended, general surveys are *The Honourable Company: a history of the English East India Company*, by John Keay (London: HarperCollins, 1991), and the lavishly illustrated *The East India Company: trade and conquest from 1600*, by Antony Wild (London: HarperCollins, 1999).

The much earlier *England's quest of Eastern trade*, by William Foster (London: A & C Black, 1933) remains a standard work for the 'foundation' period of the Company.

The trading world of Asia and the English East India Company 1660–1760, by Kirti N. Chaudhuri (Cambridge University Press, 1978) is a masterpiece of economic analysis, and the same author's *Trade and civilisation in the Indian Ocean: an economic history from the rise of Islam to 1750* (Cambridge University Press, 1985) provides a wide-ranging vision of the world which the Europeans entered.

East Indian fortunes: the British in Bengal in the eighteenth century, by Peter J. Marshall (Oxford: Clarendon Press, 1976) is essential for appreciating the impact of the 'new money'.

Lastly, there is an enormous and absolutely amazing survey of the cultural and intellectual relationships and discoveries which accompanied the trade – *Asia in the making of Europe*, by Donald F. Lach and Edwin J. Van Kley (Chicago & London: University of Chicago Press, 9 vols, 1965–93).

Index